GAMED

Why targets and incentives fail and how to fix them

GAMED

Why targets and incentives fail and how to fix them

BERNIE SMITH

MP
METRIC PRESS

Made in Sheffield
England

Published by Metric Press

60 Bromwich Road
Sheffield
S8 0GG

United Kingdom

Email: gamed@madetomeasureKPIs.com
Website: https://madetomeasureKPIs.com

First published in Great Britain in 2021

ISBN: 978-1-910047-41-5

British Library Cataloguing-in-Publication Data
A catalogue record for this book is available from the British Library
Library of Congress Cataloguing-in-Publication Data
A catalogue record for this book is available from the Library of Congress

Printed and bound in Great Britain

281021-IngS

Contents

Part 2: How to design effective targets (or fix broken ones)

Part 3: How to design effective incentives (or fix broken ones)

Part 4: Making it happen

Appendix

Thanks

Writing books is tough, particularly on those around the author. I am forever grateful to Liz, my wife, for her patience, feedback, and encouragement. Thanks also to Jon Wood for his practical insights into how people really respond to targets, to Mike Fritz for his sales know-how, and to Ariane Laurent for her proofing and editing of this book.

GAMED

Before we start

GAMED

Your free tools, templates and cheatsheets

We will be discussing and using several free tools, templates, and cheatsheets on our journey through target and incentive design. Now would be a good time to head to...

bettertargets.info

...to download your free pack, so you have them to hand as we cover them. The password you need for the download is ...

GAMED888

Who this book is for

This book is for people who:

- Are tasked with creating new, effective, performance targets, key results or incentives
- Need help fixing existing performance targets, OKRs or incentives
- Want a structured and practical design framework

This book will help you:

- Create targets and incentives that align with your strategy and deliver results
- Build engagement with your target owners
- Test your targets and incentives rigorously for unexpected outcomes and dangerous loopholes

About the author

Bernie Smith coaches businesses to develop meaningful performance measures, targets, and incentives and present their management information in the clearest possible way to support good decision making.

As the owner of Made to Measure KPIs he has worked with major organisations including Airbus, UBS, Lloyd's Register, Leonardo, Tesco Bank, Barclays, Lloyds TSB, and many others.

Previously, Bernie led teams delivering operational improvement in FTSE 100 companies using Lean and Six Sigma approaches. This took him to the US where he helped paper makers, Finland, to make olefins and Wrexham to package cheese.

Bernie lives in Sheffield, UK, with his wife Liz, two children, and some underused exercise equipment.

Introduction

Introduction

GAMED

Targets and incentives have real consequences

On Saturday, January 7th 2017 a 48 year old executive, Oliver Schmidt, was on his way home from vacation. Waiting for his flight back to Germany, in the departure lounge of Miami airport, he decided to use the men's room. As he did, the FBI arrested him, charging him with 11 felony counts, including 'Conspiracy to defraud the United States'. He was facing up to 169 years in prison.[1] His arrest, the estimated $33.3 billion of costs to his firm and the subsequent reputational damage, can be linked to aggressive EPA targets, huge potential market rewards, and the extreme behaviours they incentivised.

We will come back to Herr Schmidt in our first case study, but his story is not an isolated one. The news headlines are littered with failures that can be traced directly back to badly designed targets and incentives. Other case studies we will cover include...

- The schools that shut to improve their attendance figures.
- The medical insurance claims agents paid to make mistakes, then fix them.
- The bank sales staff incentivised to sell so recklessly that the compensation bill came to over £50 billion.

Headlines alone do not fully paint the picture of pain and frustration felt by the people in these stories. The distress that comes from being rewarded (or threatened) into doing things that just don't make sense can destroy the lives of customers, employees, and their families and puts a huge hidden burden on the whole of our society. In some cases this pain and frustration stretches over decades.

This situation can, should, and must be improved.

There are reasons to be optimistic. There are examples of targets and incentives delivering successful, sometimes stunning, outcomes:

- The eradication of smallpox.
- The repair of the ozone layer.
- A 92% reduction in single-use plastic bag consumption in the space of five years.

Effective targets also offer the only realistic management method for curtailing greenhouse gas emissions on our planet.

The prize is enormous. It _is_ possible to make targets and incentive tools for good. The question is how? To do this, we need a proper diagnosis of the disease. We need to develop a solid understanding of the many ways in which targets and incentives can go wrong.

Using that knowledge we can develop a set of systematic, repeatable methods to design effective targets and incentives, or to fix broken ones.

That is the goal of this book.

KPIs, targets, and incentives. What they are and why they are different

Before we get into the detail of target and incentive design, we need to be clear on what the terms KPI, target, and incentive mean. They are close cousins, but each has a distinct definition.

Why it's important to know the difference

Something I've noticed working with a wide range of clients is just the mention of the word 'KPI' can bring on an immediate, negative, emotional response from some people.

In almost every case, the upset person has been in a role where targets and incentives were used to drive performance outcomes, and they were heavily pressurised by their line managers and have witnessed extreme consequences for achieving or missing those targets.

In the business banking division of a very major UK retail bank, the word 'target' had actually been replaced by the word 'KPI'. Whenever the topic of 'KPIs' came up, the bank's relationship managers [sales team] often started to talk noticeably faster, with the look of hunted quarry. It took me a little while to realise that the word 'KPI' had become synonymous with either achieving your bonus or being fired. When you look at it through their eyes, their reaction seems less surprising.

It is common to use the terms KPIs, targets and incentives interchangeably, when in fact they are quite different things. As these terms are so important for this book, let's look at the difference.

What is a KPI?

A Key Performance Indicator (KPI) is a measure of how we are doing at something that we care about.

You use them every day in your personal life, probably without ever thinking of them as KPIs. The answers to questions like 'How much do I weigh?', 'How much money do I have in my bank account?', and 'How many units of alcohol have I drunk this week?' are provided by KPIs ('weight', 'bank balance', and 'units of alcohol consumed'). KPIs do not tell you whether something is good or bad, they are simply a quantified value of that thing.

A KPI is intended to provide an objective numerical value related to a specific activity or outcome.

KPIs provide an important foundation for our discussion. As the title suggests, this is a book on target and incentive design, not KPI design. If you would like to dig deeper into KPI design I'd suggest you read (or listen to) KPI Checklists. It's a good starting point for a structured approach towards KPI development and deployment.

What is a target?

It is when we compare KPIs with targets that we start to make a value judgement about whether we are performing well or poorly.

If my bathroom scales tell me I weigh 80 kg, my reaction would be shaped by my personal target. Weighing 80 kg when my target is 85 kg might be good news, less so if my target is 60 kg.

The target provides the context for reviewing our performance, as reported by our KPI values.

What is an incentive?

If KPIs provide objective numerical quantification, and targets provide the context then incentives are intended to provide behavioural motivation.

An incentive can be either positive (I buy myself a new smart watch if I hit 80 kg), negative (I will put a padlock on the fridge if I hit 85 kg) or some combination of the two.

The underlying assumption with incentives is that objective measurement, a clear target, and a suitable reward/ punishment will provide the motivation for the behavioural change required to achieve the desired outcome. This model feels intuitively reasonable to most, but as we will discover later in this book, this assumption needs to be treated with extreme caution.

It will become clear through our case studies that poorly designed incentives can be the management equivalent of throwing a bucket of gasoline on a house fire.

What tools do we currently have?

As a young child I drew stick figures with their arms emerging from the middle of their torsos, legs were shown as straight lines, and heads were circles. The sky was a thin blue strip along the top of the picture and the sun was a yellow circle. This was how I thought the world, and the people in it, were put together.

When it comes to performance targets and goal setting, the world of business seems largely stuck in the 'arms coming from the middle of body' phase of development. There are two main methods that spring to mind when you start discussing target and incentive design in modern businesses: SMART objectives and OKRs.

Whilst both approaches are widespread and popular, they do not give us everything we need to reliably create positive outcomes.

Let's take a look at the strengths and weaknesses of both approaches...

SMART goals and objectives

For many years the SMART objective setting approach was the only game in town.

The SMART approach is based on five principles identified by Locke and Latham:

1. **Clarity**: Come up with a clear goal.
2. **Challenge**: Make sure the goal is a stretch, but not impossible.
3. **Commitment**: Ensure your target owner is committed to the goal and target.
4. **Feedback**: Give regular feedback.
5. **Task complexity**: Make sure the timescale is realistic, breaking down complex tasks into sub-tasks, goals, or targets.

Perhaps CCCFT wasn't catchy enough, so it evolved into SMART, which stands for 'Specific, Measurable, Achievable, Realistic, and Time-bound' (there are a few alternatives for the A, R & T).

All five principles are valid, yet it is perfectly possible to design a target that ticks all five boxes but does not deliver the expected results and outcomes in the real world.

Strengths of SMART goal setting

- SMART is easy to remember, intuitive, and easy to explain and understand.
- It is a checklist, so requires little effort to follow.
- It is applicable to any situation.

Weaknesses of SMART goal setting

- There is no attempt to anticipate negative consequences or behaviours.
- The steps are not broken down — what constitutes 'achievable' for example?
- There is no attempt to link the SMART goal with an overarching strategic objective.

- SMART only applies to <u>target setting</u>, and does not offer any guidance on incentive design.

Locke and Latham's five principles and SMART goal-setting are a solid start, but definitely do not fully prepare us for what will happen to our carefully created targets in the wild. The behaviours that targets drive are just too complex to be covered in five brief bullet points.

As we pick through the case studies in Part 1, you may be struck by just how many of the targets and incentives meet the SMART checklist points and yet still failed.

OKRs - Objective Key Results

If you haven't come across them already OKR is a goal-setting approach pioneered in Intel, based on Peter Drucker's work on Management by Objectives in the 1950s, which is now used widely across the corporate world. OKR stands for 'Objective Key Results'.

The **Objective** element describes a substantial, often long-term outcome we want to achieve.

The **Key Result** is a smaller outcome, a stepping stone goal, that will help us reach that big 'Objective'.

An example personal OKR

Objective: Give up smoking

Key Result: Go 10 days without a cigarette

An example corporate OKR

Objective: Quadruple online sales

Key Result: Grow email list to 50k subscribers

Strengths of the OKR approach

The OKR approach is powerful, flexible, and gloriously simple to explain. Translating OKR into the language of this book, both the Objective and Key Results are <u>targets</u>. We need to know how we are progressing on our Objectives and Key Results, so each Key Result is accompanied by a KPI to indicate progress.

Weaknesses of the OKR approach

The OKR approach does not offer:

- Guidance on whether those targets will deliver the intended higher-level strategic outcome.
- Indication of likely 'gaming' by the OKR owners.
- Identification of unintended consequences.

Like SMART objectives, the OKR approach only covers target setting and offers no guidance on incentive design.

The approach we share in this book, the ROKET-DS™ method, is not only fully compatible with the OKR approach, it is a powerful <u>addition</u> to the OKR methodology.

Using OKRs and ROKET-DS together

The thinking behind OKRs and ROKET-DS™ is in complete alignment, so you might be thinking, "OK Bernie, if OKRs are so great, why did you need to write this book?" Well, there are four areas where ROKET-DS™ extends and enhances the OKR approach:

How ROKET-DS™ <u>enhances</u> the OKR approach

1. OKR evangelists often talk about the importance of 'alignment of goals', 'setting stretch targets', and 'building engagement'. In practice, there is little built-in to the stock OKR method offering specific guidance on how to do this. ROKET-DS™ provides detailed step-by-step practical guidance on every step of the target development process, from start to finish.

2. The stock OKR methodology does not explore how targets will be gamed, circumvented, and corrupted nor how to avoid this happening. In ROKET-DS™ we go through a rigorous process of analysing target-owner agency, white-hat, and black-hat testing.

How ROKET-DS™ <u>extends</u> OKR methodology

1. ROKET-DS™ has been engineered to support the design of both one-off objectives (missions) and everyday 'business as usual' targets and incentives. OKRs are unashamedly project based. They have a finite life, existing only until the outcome is delivered, then they need to be replaced or reworked. Individual OKRs are not designed or intended for long-term 'business as usual management'.

2. The OKR approach does not cover <u>incentive</u> design. ROKET-DS™ is designed to integrate the target and incentive design process in one seamless method.

In short, OKRs are an awesome tool, but many people need more detail regarding implementation, guidance on how to create 'business as usual targets', and an integrated approach to designing incentives. This is where our ROKET-DS™ approach can help. Although the terminology is a little different, the first part of our system, the ROKET-DS™ Target Design process, is <u>directly applicable</u> to setting meaningful OKRs.

A word of caution, this will take a little commitment

One of the reasons that OKRs and SMART objectives have become so dominant is that they are simple and easy to explain. That's great, but what's not so positive is that neither method offers much help when it comes to designing human-centric targets and incentives.

Anyone who has played a board game with friends and family will know that, when the stakes are high, people are fantastically creative and devious. No simplistic system can deliver robust and reliable targets and incentives. It's going to take some work, a few iterations, and some patience.

What I can promise is that if you follow the steps in the book, you will come up with something better, more reliable, and easier to explain than any of the alternative methods. If you focus your new skills on the right target, there is also a very real chance you will transform your performance, forever. Worth the effort? I would think so.

Use it or lose it: Choose a project to work on as you go

The method we cover in Part 2 will only work if you <u>apply</u> it. To keep you focused on the end-game, I suggest you think of at least one real-life application for this method right now, so you can apply each of the steps as we work through them. This will work best if you choose a target to develop that is...

- Very significant to the performance of your business or organisation
- Has a people-performance element to it
- Something you will also want to pair with an incentive

Once you have decided on your 'special project', just print out the ROKET-DS™ Target Canvas for Part 2 and the ROKET-DS™ Incentive Canvas for Part 3 and you are all set.

I will give you a gentle nudge to apply each step to your own project as we work through the method in Parts 2 and 3.

Introduction

GAMED

Part 1: How and why targets and incentives go wrong

Failure case studies

When I started to investigate the real-world problems with targets and incentives it became clear that similar target and incentive issues appeared time and again. There was a pattern. Years of professional problem-solving has taught me that where there is a 'pattern of failure' you can normally use a structured, repeatable process to fix those failures. This analysis eventually led to the Results-Orientated KPI Effective Target Design System (ROKET-DS™).

In this section we will carefully dissect several high-profile case studies, teasing out the common issues that can be used to help diagnose targets and incentive design problems in any situation. These case studies are a hand-picked subset of the ones I used to develop the ROKET-DS™ method. We will get to grips with the ROKET-DS™ method itself in Part 2 of this book.

If you just want to 'get to the method' then you can safely jump ahead to **Part 2: How to design effective targets** or **Part 3: How to design effective incentives**, but if you are curious, or just enjoy hearing about barely believable self-inflicted organisational chaos, I suggest you read on.

The case studies in this section include ambulance service targets, where a death could be reported as a success; a motor racing class, where the rules were stretched to the absurd; mutual funds that could discreetly forget their failures when reporting performance; schools which were shut to improve attendance figures; a medical insurance claims processor who was paid to make mistakes and then paid even more to fix them; and a national school exam system that saw a 196% increase in top grades over a 40 year period. We will finish with a fictional case study that encapsulates some of the most useful research on performance **incentives** in a digestible format.

As we work our way through these case studies, we will build up a kind of 'encyclopaedia of problems' which we call the ROKET-DS™ Diagnostic. You will find a reference example for each failure type in the Appendix (and in your downloads pack) along with a failure description, why it is important and a simple example.

Diesel Defeat

The facts and events in this example are based on publicly available information.

We opened this book with the unfortunate story of Oliver Schmidt. To recap...

On Saturday, January 7th 2017 a 48 year old executive, Oliver Schmidt, was on his way home from vacation. Waiting for his flight back to Germany, in the departure lounge of Miami airport, he decided to use the men's room. As he did, the FBI arrested him, charging him with 11 felony counts, including 'Conspiracy to defraud the United States'. He faced up to 169 years in prison.

How did it come to this?

Schmidt's misfortune can be traced back to two things.

Firstly, the attractiveness of the North American automobile market. European manufacturers saw that diesel engine vehicles had only 5% market penetration in the US, compared with 50% in their home market. Diesel automobiles have better fuel economy potential than gasoline versions, coupled with great drivability, so manufacturers saw a tremendous prize.

The second issue was the targets set in the Clean Air Act, US legislation intended to reduce air pollution through aggressively low emissions targets. A major focus of these targets is on NOx levels, nitrogen oxides, which are linked to a number of health problems in those exposed to them. The US NOx emissions targets are significantly lower than the European ones. Meeting NOx targets for diesel engines is tougher still. Catalytic converters worked well for petrol engines, but different technology was needed for diesel engines to hit the tough 0.043g/km NOx limit set by the US

Environmental Protection Agency (EPA). BMW had developed an effective system, based on urea additives (known as AdBlue), but it was bulky, expensive, and high-maintenance. Instead, VW Audi had decided to pursue 'Lean NOx trap' technology, which would be cheaper and easier to implement.

There was just one problem. The 'Lean NOx trap' technology did not work well enough. VW Audi struggled to develop an engine which met the EPA emissions targets, was drivable, and gave acceptable fuel economy.

Why did VW Audi do this?

Diesel cars are more expensive than petrol cars to start with. Adding expensive emissions control systems would only nudge the price tag further in the wrong direction, jeopardising their bold push into the US market. Faced with a tough choice, VW Audi decided to cheat. They did this by reverse-engineering the emissions testing process. They programmed the engine control unit (ECU) in their cars to identify the exact conditions that indicated the vehicle was on an emissions test rig — based on the position of the steering wheel, air pressure and duration of operation.[2] They then embedded special code, dubbed a 'defeat device', in the ECU firmware to put the engine in an 'emissions test mode' when testing was detected. In this mode, the ECU would dramatically alter the characteristics of the engine. An engine in 'emissions test mode' would be virtually un-drivable in the real world, but enabled VW Audi cars to pass the test. VW Audi secretly introduced this technology to the US market in 2009, selling over 500,000 Audis with defeat devices in the US alone.

Oliver Schmidt oversaw the VW Audi emission office in Michigan and was alleged to be deeply involved in VW's attempts to game the emissions standards, to cover up the crime and, later, in their attempt to concoct alternative benign explanations for their emission failures.

How was the con uncovered?

Many Audi diesel owners noticed a build-up of soot around the exhaust outlets of their Audis, but were assured that the emissions were normal by their dealers. The deception only came to light when a group of scientists at West Virginia University, funded by the ICCT (International Council on Clean Transportation) decided to run 'real world driving' tests on three diesel cars: a Volkswagen Passat, a Volkswagen Jetta, and a BMW X5. Using a 'portable emissions measurement system' (PEMS) to measure on-the-road emissions, things started to unravel for VW Audi. After thousands of kilometres of testing, the BMW was found to be 'at or below standard... with the exception of rural-up/downhill driving conditions' and the Jetta was found to be exceeding limits by 'a factor of 15 to 35' and the Passat 'by a factor of 5 to 20'[3]. The game was up, though VW Audi did not come quietly:

> "After a study by West Virginia University first raised questions over Volkswagen's diesel motors in early 2014, Mr. Schmidt played a central role in trying to convince regulators that excess emissions were caused by technical problems rather than by deliberate cheating," Ian Dinsmore, an F.B.I. agent, said in a sworn affidavit used as the basis for Mr. Schmidt's arrest.
>
> *New York Times, Jan 9 2017*

For more than a year, VW repeatedly floated 'alternative' technical theories for the high emissions levels before finally formally admitting the existence of the defeat devices in September 2015.

The impact and the cost to VW Audi

Under threat of withheld approval for VW Audi's 2016 models by the EPA[4] , in 2015 VW Audi announced plans to offer to refit around 11 million affected vehicles. For some this took the form of a ECU software update, for other vehicles it was a hardware upgrade. Some owners were offered buybacks and others were offered compensation.

In addition to the impact on health, which was estimated to be around 59 premature deaths[5] for the US, the whole episode cost VW Audi an estimated $33.3 billion (by June 2020)[6] , a sales drop of 24% in the US, and a severely damaged reputation.

For Oliver Schmidt, the impact was a seven-year federal jail sentence and a $400k fine.

'Diesel defeat' study issues and failure types

As we work through our case studies, we will recap the key features of each study and tease out the shared, underlying issues. Each new issue will be given a reference code, for example IF-02, which you can use to locate a full description in the Appendix. These numbered generic issue types will form part of our diagnostic toolkit later on.

Key features, issues, and failure types (in bold) from this study:

- A large, potentially lucrative, market for diesel cars in the US with low penetration numbers. **Extreme reward or punishment IF-02**

- Apparent focus on sales and market penetration targets above all else. **Intense management pressure MF-03**

- Ultimately, the entire episode was highly damaging to VW Audi and yet individuals apparently felt encouraged to pursue the 'defeat device' approach. **Individual and organisational success not aligned TF-08**
- Very high stakes, $500-$1000 additional cost per car associated with fitting the superior AdBlue emissions control solution. **Extreme reward or punishments IF-02**
- Serious legal consequences of being caught. **Extreme reward or punishments IF-02**
- Inadequate method of measuring target compliance. **Weak enforcement MF-01** and **Using loopholes DB-04**
- Transparent testing method enabled 'gaming'. **Using loopholes DB-04** and **User input misclassification DB-05**
- The real-world emissions were far higher than intended by the regulators. **Unexpected adverse outcomes DB-06**
- Opaque software prevented scrutiny (the defeat device was mislabelled as an 'acoustic condition' in the code)[7]. **Rule bending or breaking DB-03** and **Breaking the law DB-02**

Chronic Complaint

Ambulance Service targets designed for failure

The facts and events in this example are based on publicly available information.

The situation

In 1974 the British ambulance service decided that it needed a way to track its effectiveness in dealing with incidents. To achieve this, they devised a set of KPIs and targets. The result was a system called ORCON (Operational Research CONsultancy).

This system set out a number of KPIs and targets, the primary one being that 75% of calls designated as 'life-threatening' (Category A) should 'receive an initial response within 8 minutes and 95% within 19 minutes'. These were known as the A8 and A19 targets.

For 43 years the ORCON A8 and A19 targets became the laser focus of ambulance services throughout the UK, to such an extent that it was sometimes referred to as 'The Lord God ORCON' or the 'Cult of ORCON' by those in the ambulance service.

The principle behind these targets seemed logical. If you can respond rapidly to clinically urgent incidents the patient should have a better chance of survival. Unfortunately, these good intentions resulted in highly dysfunctional behaviour, encouraged cheating, and often ignored patient wellbeing.

The problems with ORCON

It didn't matter what happened to the patient

The 8-minute target took no account of the <u>outcome</u> of the incident. So an A8 call reached within 9 minutes, where the patient was helped to survive a heart attack would be regarded as a failure and another A8 patient collected in 7 minutes but already dead for an hour would be regarded as a success. The target promoted response time without considering the clinical outcomes.

The 8-minute target had no basis in medicine

Brain death typically occurs around 5 minutes after oxygen deprivation (at normal temperatures), whilst something serious like trauma does need urgent treatment but has what is called 'the golden hour' in which treatment is likely to be effective. No evidence seems to exist for the validity of the 8 minute target, it appears to be an arbitrary figure.

It builds a 25% failure rate into the target.

The ORCON targets profoundly shaped the psychology of the ambulance service operations team. This quote from Matthew Westhorpe's blog (former paramedic and now a clinical adviser with the NHS 111 service) gives you a feel for how seriously the 75% target was taken:

> *East of England Ambulance Service boasted that it had 'smashed' the 75% target. It achieved 76.9% in September of 2011. Apparently 1.9% in one month constitutes a smashing and Chief Executive Hayden Newton was said to be 'thrilled'. Not a mention was given to the 23.1% of calls that failed to be attended within time, nor was it clear what the final outcomes were of those 76.9% of attendances. It didn't matter, for one month, the Cult of ORCON had achieved ambulance perfection.*
>
> *Westhorpe, Matthew. The Cult of ORCON. https://westhorpe. net/2012/10/the-cult-of-orcon/*

How ORCON went wrong

The design created potentially corrupting pressures

Faced with a choice between a critical patient who might take 10 minutes to reach or a less serious case, on the cusp of the A8-A19 boundary, which could be reached in 8 minutes, there is a clear systemic driver to categorise the second case as an A8 and so prioritising it.

The targets system encouraged dirty tricks and manipulation

- Faced with a call that could likely not be reached within 8 minutes, the call handler may feel under pressure to downgrade the seriousness of the call, categorising a borderline case as A19 rather than A8.
- Ambulance services sometimes dispatched up to four vehicles to a patient in an attempt to meet the 8 minute target.[8]

- A single manned car would sometimes be dispatched to a serious incident, with no ability to offer transportation, which was then counted as a 'success', whilst motorbikes and pushbikes were specifically excluded from being a valid response to A19 calls.

In 2017, one in four patients needing hospital treatment experienced a 'hidden wait', where the vehicle dispatched, a bike or a car, was not able to transport the patient to A&E (accident and emergency).[9]

- As the call handling time was included in the response time, it pressured call handlers to rush through the call, potentially leading to the wrong care being delivered (e.g., stroke victims not being taken straight to a specialist stroke unit) or calls being miscategorised.
- The minimum requirement for a working ambulance is a roadworthy vehicle and a bag-valve-mask and defibrillator[10] — this low basic requirement encouraged services to send out under-equipped ambulances just to meet the ORCON targets.

The targets affected staff morale

Ambulance Service staff were confronted with the unintended effects of the ORCON targets on a daily basis for over four decades. The ORCON targets created high levels of frustration and anger, let patients down or delivered potentially poor outcomes.

> *We are hideously overused and understaffed, we face delays at hospital owing to overcrowding and delays on-scene because of the ignorant people we have to attend to. None of this matters – all that matters is the 8 minute deadline. If we make 75% of all calls in 8 minutes we get more money from the government, which means more staff, vehicles that work etc...*

> *Reynolds, Tom. Blood, Sweat and Tea,. HarperCollins*

Half of all 999 calls were not covered by the targets

In 2017 half of all ambulance calls, around five million a year, are classed as 'green' and were not covered by any national target. Response times for these patients, who were often frail and elderly, could be 6 hours or longer.

Death of 'The cult of ORCON'

After 43 years of ORCON, a new set of ambulance standards was implemented in England. A major study by Sheffield University published in 2013 led to an overhaul of the targets of the ambulance service in 2017. This included:

- New questions to assess the urgency of response required.
- More time for the call handlers to assess the calls.
- Four incident categories were introduced (along with new assessment questions), with targets which are more appropriate for the urgency of each category.

Category 1

Life threatening, urgent calls (e.g., heart attack) — new target average response time of 7 minutes. The 'clock' will only stop when the most appropriate vehicle reaches the scene, not just the first to arrive.

Category 2

Emergency calls (e.g., stroke) — new target average response time of 18 minutes.

Category 3

Urgent problems, such as an uncomplicated diabetic issue, which requires treatment and transport to an acute setting — at least 9 out of 10 times within 120 minutes.

Category 4

Least urgent calls, stable clinical cases requiring transportation — at least 9 out of 10 times within 180 minutes.

Key improvements of the new system over the old

Using average response times

A service like the ambulance service will inevitably be affected by factors such as traffic, weather, and geography (some incidents may be more remote than others). Using an average, rather than a 'pass/ fail' score, gives a more balanced view of the performance. Of course, extreme outliers should be reviewed and investigated if necessary.

Not building failure into the target

A 75% achievement of an 8 minute response built an assumed failure rate of up to 25% into a 'successful' service. The use of an average score on 100% of calls in each category ends this nonsense.

The most urgent conditions get their own targets

Heart attacks and strokes have specific targets that cover the time from the start of the call to the time they received definitive treatment.

The least urgent calls finally have targets too

For the least serious calls, Category 4, there is now a target of 90% of calls being transported within 180 mins. Whilst a potential wait of 180 mins is a long one, it is an improvement over the untargeted waits of 6+ hours under the ORCON system.

'Chronic complaint' study issues and failure types

Key features, issues, and problem types from this study:

- The 8 minute target appears arbitrary. **Arbitrary target selection TF-07**
- The performance targets were in no way linked to patient outcome. **Weak/no link to intended positive outcome TF-06**
- Striving to achieve the target could have an adverse impact on patient outcomes, in some circumstances. **Unexpected adverse outcomes DB-06**
- The 8 and 19 minute targets were 'Pass or fail' targets on each call, not averages. **All or nothing TF-01**

- The ORCON rules created a potential risk of call handlers to downgrading borderline 'no hope' calls from A8 to A19. **User input misclassification DB-05**

- Up to four ambulances would be sent to A8 calls that would be a 'stretch' to reach in 8 minutes. **Resource fire-hosing DB-09**

- Targets rewarded the use of legal but very lightly equipped vehicles. **Rule bending or breaking DB-03** and **Using loopholes DB-04**

High-stakes for hitting or missing overall targets...

- Insiders regularly talked of very high levels of pressure to achieve ORCON targets. **Intense management pressure MF-03**

- Funding was often based on ORCON performance. **Extreme reward or punishment IF-02**

- There was a perception amongst ambulance crew members that the ORCON targets took precedence over patient well-being in the minds of their senior managers. **Negative leadership behaviour role-modelling MF-02**

- Paramedics, like many caring professions, are often strongly driven by **intrinsic motivation**. The highly visible, chronically-unaddressed issues with the ORCON targets damaged motivation for many. **Apathy, cynicism DB-10**

Targets alone do not fix operational problems

Just getting the targets right (sensible, fair, and safe) will not fix the underlying operational issues — it simply provides a measure of achievement. Many of the problems that the Ambulance service experienced may be symptoms of wider issues, such as reduced access to out-of-hours care, an ageing population and a general increase in the need for urgent healthcare. Simply attaching ever more extreme rewards or penalties to the target performance will not fix these issues — the service itself also needs adequate funding and management.

Family Friendly Motoring

The facts and events in this example are based on publicly available information.

Motor racing has classes, lots of classes. Each class has specific rules and regulations. In 1995 Toyota decided to enter a custom built car for a class know as 'Production-based GT', governed by the GT1 rules. Their car was called the Toyota GT-One.

The production-based class required a small number of production cars be offered for sale. There was another requirement too. The intent was that GT cars would be 'usable' by members of the public, so the rules stipulated that each GT car must have a storage space capable of holding a 'standard sized suitcase'.

Toyota, like all entrants, was obliged to follow the rules. They identified two important loopholes.

Firstly, there was no lower limit on the number of cars on offer to the public. So their run of cars available to the public was.... two cars, both of which ended up in motor museums.

Secondly, they realised there were no regulations on the accessibility or practicality of the 'suitcase sized storage space'. Toyota managed to convince the governing body (Automobile Club de l'Ouest) that the GT-One's fuel tank, which would be empty when the car was examined by the race inspector, was allowable trunk space as it could theoretically hold a suitcase.

Toyota produced a car that fully complied with the letter of the regulations, but bore no resemblance to the obvious intent, that the cars on the track represented real cars that spectators could buy and use themselves.

'Family friendly motoring' study issues and failure types

Key features, issues and problem types from this study:

- It's a race, so it's all about winning — 'Second is the fastest loser' mentality. **Winner takes all outcome IF-04** and **All or nothing TF-01**

- Lax definitions. Clearly the creators of the race did not intend for fuel tanks to be used as a storage space for luggage, but the rules did not prohibit this leading to 'creative' interpretation of those rules. **Incomplete rule definition TF-02, Rule bending or breaking DB-03** and **Using loophole DB-04**

- Lack of functional test — a requirement to stow a case, within a certain period of time, without using tools would have disallowed Toyota's dubious solution. **Weak enforcement MF-01**

- The competitors had no interest or investment in the spirit of the rules — a concept described as 'moral disengagement'. **Negative leadership behaviour role-modelling MF-02**

Mutual Fund Madness

How funds trick customers by burying their dead

The facts and events in this example are based on publicly available information.

Past performance is no guarantee of future results

Surely 'make more money' is a target no-one can dodge? Actively managed mutual funds are financial products where investors give their cash to a fund manager, who then actively manages a portfolio of investments on the investor's behalf. The idea is that this kind of management, in expert hands, can outperform more pedestrian forms of investment management, creating a healthy return for the investor and a well-paid job for the fund manager. As of 2019, more than $15 trillion was invested this way.[11]

Showing attractive returns is an essential requirement for funds to survive and attract more investors.

You might think that there's nowhere to hide when it comes to selling funds to customers. Surely it's a pretty straightforward question of looking at the fund's performance to determine how well it's done in the past?

It turns out there are actually a number of tricks an unscrupulous fund manager can use to make their performance look better than it really is. They do this using 'survival bias'. Here's how it works...

Over a 15 year period, 58.5% of US-based actively managed funds were closed or merged into other funds.[12] Most commonly, this happens because the fund is not performing well.

When a fund is closed or merged into another fund, the data on the fund is normally excluded from future performance reporting, giving a false, rosy picture, based only on the performance of the surviving funds. It's as though the poor performers never existed.

If you want to see the impact of this 'selective amnesia', let's take a look at some 2017 data from SPIVA U.S. Scorecard....

Over a 15 year period just 13.8% of multi-cap growth funds beat their benchmarks.

But, if a data provider excludes the performance of closed funds, the percentage of funds beating their benchmarks shoots up to 43%.

There is no industry standard on how to report closed and merged funds, so of course funds will report their performance in the most favourable way.

This effect, hiding your failures, is called 'survival bias' and can create a very distorted view of performance. (In our system, we call the behaviour that creates this survival bias 'User input misclassification'.)

So, next time you see a fund boasting about the performance of its star product, you might want to consider the potential graveyard of failed funds from that seller which were quietly buried without a headstone.

'Mutual fund madness' study issues and failure types

Key features, issues, and problem types from this study:

- Funds use 'survival bias' to bury bad performances. **Design input bias TF-03**
- There is a powerful relationship between strong reported historic fund performance and attracting new customers. **Extreme reward or punishment IF-02**

- The reporting approach used by funds reduces the trustworthiness of reported historic performance, an example of **Corrupted reporting DB-08**

- If a fund buyer expects future performance in line with reported historic performance, they could be in for a nasty surprise. **Unexpected adverse outcomes DB-06**

- A lack of regulation on how to report historic performance demonstrates **Weak enforcement MF-01** and **Incomplete rule definition TF-02**

Medical Mayhem

How a medical insurer tied itself in knots using targets

This case study is loosely based on a real-world situation. Names, details and figures have been changed.

The story

A sizeable (in excess of £2bn) medical insurer, let's call them 'Kako Healthcare', decided to outsource its claims handling to a major third-party professional service provider, who we will call 'Amblys Services' for anonymity.

Under the contractual arrangement between the two companies, Kako would pass the treatment claims to Amblys to review, process, and pay, if approved.

Amblys were compensated at £5 per claim handled. Amblys built their business model to maximise revenue so each claim handling clerk had targets for the number of claims they processed per hour. The trouble is, when a claim is rejected, the clerk needs to provide a detailed explanation as to why, and handle pushback from hospitals and patients where claims were rejected. As a result, it was much faster to pay a claim than reject it.

Impact: This combination of targets and process design meant that Amblys were incentivised to approve and pay invalid claims.

It gets worse...

Invoices from hospitals would often include duplicate and inappropriate charges. Here's one example...

Hospitals often have a 'bundle' agreement with Kako, where the pre-op is covered in the agreed cost of surgery. Sometimes hospitals would invoice for the pre-op in addition to the bundle-surgery fee, double-invoicing the pre-op fees. Are the claims handlers going to take the time to review patient history to detect these duplicates? No, not when they are targeted and rewarded for handling claims quickly. As a result, duplicate invoices were frequently authorised by Amblys without being detected.

Impact: The productivity targets were incentivising Amblys staff to ignore duplicate invoicing.

...and worse still...

This 'duplicated invoice issue' was flagged by a Kako improvement team, working to reduce inappropriate claims payments. Fortunately, all Kako contracts allowed a period where they could claim back inappropriate payments from hospitals. They put a remediation team in place to recover those payments. That team was very, very successful.

The Kako accountants looked at the cost of the remediation team and thought, "Couldn't Amblys do this at a lower cost?"

Amblys, their prime outsourcing contractor, offered a lower price and won the remediation contract.

To incentivise Amblys to find erroneously paid claims, Kako agreed that Amblys could keep 10% of the 'savings'. The average claim recovery was £100 per claim, so Kako kept £90 with Amblys getting £10 for their efforts. It was very successful — Amblys found many invalid claims and everyone was happy (especially Amblys).

Impact: Amblys were directly profiting through detecting and correcting mistakes they made (and were rewarded for) in the first place.

'Medical mayhem' study issues and failure types

Key features, issues, and problem types from this study:

- The productivity target, coupled with the extra process time and effort for a rejected claim, incentivised the Amblys team to approve cases that were not valid. **Output misclassification DB-07** and **Unexpected adverse outcomes DB-06**

- Agents were incentivised <u>not</u> to enforce claim-rules rigorously or correctly. **Rule bending or breaking DB-03** and **Invisible bar-lowering DB-01**

- Agent reward was linked solely to throughput, not accuracy or profitability. **Weak/no link to intended positive outcome TF-06**

- Amblys then directly profited from finding and fixing the 'mistakes' it had been incentivised to make. **Individual and (client) organisational success not aligned TF-08**

- There was no separation between 'error creation' and 'error detection and remediation', and the rewards for fixing the errors compounded this conflict of interest. **Weak rule enforcement MF-01** and **Negative behaviour role-modelling MF-02**

A-Grade Abundance

The facts and events in this example are based on publicly available information.

A-levels are a qualification typically studied by UK students over two years between the age of 16 and 18. A-levels are used as both a school leaving certificate and university entrance qualification. Each year 700,000–800,000 students sit A-level exams.

UK A-level results, by grade 1989-2016

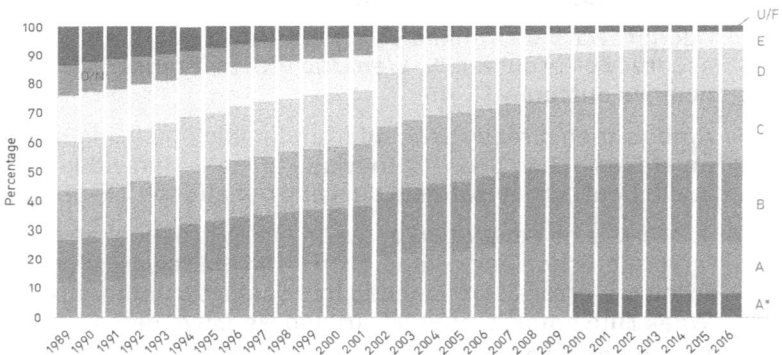

Source: Wikipedia - 'Grade Inflation'[13]

Over the period 1989 to 2009 there was a 134% increase in the number of students achieving the top A grade. In recognition of this, a new more challenging grade of A* was introduced to allow the most able students to be identified.

In parallel, there was a near 13-fold drop in fail grades (grades O, N, U and F), dropping from 24.3% of entrants in 1989 to 1.9% in 2016.

This pattern of grade inflation is mirrored in the awarding of top grades at degree level (1st class degree awards), increasing from 8.4% in 1994 to 28.4% in 2019.

This issue is not confined to the UK...

- In France, between 2005 and 2016, the proportion of students receiving an honour in the General Baccalauréat doubled.
- In India a '95% aggregate' CBSE score was 21 times more prevalent in 2017 than it was in 2004.[14]

...and is not a recent phenomenon...

- Research by Professor Louis Goldman (Wichita State University), looking at 134 US colleges, showed an increase in Grade Point Average (GPA) of 0.404 between 1965 and 1975, with GPA measured on a scale between 0.0 and 4.0.

'A-grade abundance' study issues and failure types

Key features, issues, and problem types from this study:

- A-level grades determine whether students secure a place at their preferred university. **Extreme reward or punishment IF-02**
- The A-level system moved away from 'grade distribution' where a fixed percentage of any given grade is awarded leading to a risk of **Invisible bar-lowering DB-01** and increasing the pressure on moderation.
- Exam boards operate in competition with each other. An exam board that grades 'generously' is attractive to schools looking to maximise their results (benefiting their league-table ranking).This has created significant and persistent upward pressure on grading. **Intense management pressure MF-03**. This competition also brings the risk of **Invisible bar-lowering DB-01** and **Intentional bar lowering TF-05**

- Universities that boast a high percentage of 1st class degrees have a market advantage in attracting fee-paying students. **Intense management pressure MF-03** and **Extreme reward or punishment IF-02**

- It is possible that some of top-grade increase has been as a result of improvements in teaching or student ability, but it is unlikely to fully explain the level of grade inflation seen.

- The reduction in 'fails' at A-level (grades U /F and O/N prior to 2002) is likely to be the result of 'design input bias' where schools choose not to enter weak candidates for public exams in a bid to improve their grade average. This may also be a factor in the increased <u>proportion</u> of higher grades — those expected to achieve lower grades persuaded (or prevented) from sitting the exams at all. **Design input bias TF-03**

Software Sales Shenanigans

This is a fictional story based on several, separate real-world examples given by software sales professionals. All names, identifying details and figures have been changed.

Now we come to incentives. There's plenty of research on the topic of incentives, particularly sales incentives, by academics including Thomas Steenburgh, Noah Lim, Sanjog Misra, and Harikesh Nair. It's difficult to develop our incentives ruleset from case studies so we're going to lean heavily on that science and research to derive our incentive design principles. Having said that, a fictional case study can still be useful for explaining how these theories fit together. This case study will be shared in two parts. In this chapter we will set the scene at our fictional software vendor 'Shizzle Systems' and in Part 3 of this book we will close the story arc by discussing how their many problems were resolved.

Simon Shenanigans was an ambitious sales executive with a mid-sized software vendor, let's call them Shizzle Systems.

Shizzle were keen to grow their share of the manufacturing materials planning software market for their core product: Sharlatan Scheduling 3.0.

Shizzle introduced a sales incentive program for their sales team. Simon and the rest of the sales team had an allotted territory and were rewarded as follows:

- They were offered 7% of the Annual Contract Value (ACV) for contracts signed-off by close of business, on the last day of any given quarter if their ACV sales for that month exceeded $300k.
- So if Simon sells $299k he gets nothing, if he sells $301k, he receives a bonus of $21k.

To qualify for the bonus, he must also make at least 30 sales calls a week and log those calls correctly in the CRM system.

Two weeks from the end of his third quarter Simon is having a bad time of it. All of his leads seem to be mired in delay. To make things worse, he is also very behind on his calls. With two weeks to go, his sales stand at $87k and it is starting to look like he is going to miss his targets.

Here's how Simon managed to save his bonus and his new kitchen...

Firstly he needed to hit his sales call target, which he is very behind on. To do this he decided to invent a good reason for a quick call to each of his customers, whilst avoiding getting bogged-down in long discussions. He decided to ring to 'check he has the correct contact address details' so that the Christmas hamper from Shizzle Systems finds its way to the right person. After a couple of afternoons 'playing Father Christmas' he was back on track with his calls. The CRM showed the right number of outbound calls to the clients on his list, so that part of his bonus was covered.

Next, he needed to fix his sales shortfall. To do this, he decided to focus on his biggest lead, Cyberdine Security Systems. He reviewed his sales notes to remind himself of the key details...

- Cyberdine have been sitting on a $120k ACV (Annual Contract Value) proposal, for a Sharlatan 3.0 implementation across their Canadian sites, for nearly three months.

- Cyberdine is concerned that Sharlatan 3.0 will not connect to their ageing ERP system. They are asking for a custom built connector.

- Cyberdine are also considering Shizzle's forecasting product, Feckless Forecast 3.5, and have provisionally budgeted spend for the next financial year.

- Cyberdine have sites in Canada (Simon's territory), but also the UK and India. They are considering rolling Sharlatan 3.0 out to those sites too.

Simon saw his opportunity, but the current proposal for $150k ACV was not big enough to hit his target. To get Cyberdine 'over the line' he decided to...

- Offer to roll-in licenses for the UK and India into the contract for just a $50k/annum premium, on the condition that the invoice is paid through the Canadian division of the client so it will count as 'his territory'.
- Discount the full price of the maintenance contract by 50% for the first 3 years, as long as the client does it as a rebate, so he can invoice the full value initially. Rebates are not counted against his ACV value.
- Throw-in the Feckless Forecast 3.5 product at a 50% discount.
- Agree to develop a custom connector to Cyberdine's ageing 'Terminator' ERP system.
- Promised to go live in 3 months from sign-off, instead of the implementation team's estimate of 6 months (an estimate which did not include the development of the new connector).

...as long as the client signed off the contract. They did, and Simon smashed his sales target, signing off $450k for that quarter. But what was the real price to Shizzle?

In his desperation to hit his targets, Simon...

- Gamed his call targets, making calls to hit the target, but with no serious attempt to develop those contacts.
- Poached sales from India and UK sales regions, on the technicality that the billing is going through his territory, but offering a huge effective discount in doing so.
- Given away 50% of the value of the maintenance contract for three years, exploiting an ACV (Annual Contract Value) loophole that does include rebates to arrive at a net ACV.

- Discounted Feckless Forecast 3.5 below cost, to pull the sale forward to the current quarter, effectively 'borrowing from the future'.
- Committed the development team to developing a connector for an obscure, obsolete, ERP system, with costs and risks that come with custom development, at no cost to Cyberdine.
- Committed to an impossibly tight implementation schedule, even excluding the time needed for custom connector development.

In summary, Simon sold the entire package with zero assessment of profitability, operational risk, or capacity. He stole sales from his colleagues, his future self, and made expensive promises that others would have to honour. It is very likely that the systems will be delivered late and incomplete.

We will return to Shizzle Systems and how they fixed their issues in Part 3: Shizzle Sales Incentives Case Study.

'Software sales shenanigans' study issues and failure types

Key features, issues, and problem types from this study:

- Targeting 'sales calls made' is using activity as a proxy for results. Simply making calls in no way guarantees sales results. **Weak/no link to intended positive outcome TF-06** and **Arbitrary target selection TF-07**
- The sales team are not targeted on profitability, just sales value (ACV, annual contract value, in this example), leading to the sales team being rewarded for contracts that make a loss. **Individual and organisational success not aligned TF-08**

- The ACV goal was 'all or nothing', driving the team members to desperate measures to hit or exceed the target threshold. **All or nothing TF-01**

The use of do-or-die quarterly targets encouraged...

- 'Stealing from the next quarter'. **User input misclassification DB-05**
- 'Poaching clients' from other members of the team. **Rule bending or breaking DB-03** and **Using loopholes DB-04**
- 'Boomerang' sales, in this case using a rebate on the maintenance contract. **Using loopholes DB-04**

The sales team had no interest in operational practicality, leading to...

- Unrealistic delivery deadlines being agreed, to land the contract. **Inappropriate timescale TF-10**
- Potentially undeliverable feature promises being made (the ERP connector development). **Individual and organisational success not aligned TF-08**
- Likely customer dissatisfaction with systems that will be delivered late and missing critical functionality. **Unexpected adverse outcomes DB-06**

Targeted Truancy

The facts and events in this example are based on publicly available information.

Most people agree that missing school is not good for children. Many governments focus on measuring and reducing unauthorised pupil absences — truancy.

Sometimes there are legitimate reasons why children cannot attend school. One such reason is snow. A singular focus on truancy backfired spectacularly in the UK as The Telegraph newspaper explained in this article.[15]

> *Pupils unable to get into school because of snow had been listed as unauthorised absences – hitting a school's truancy figures. This often made it easier for a school to close completely.*

So, when bad weather prevented some children getting to school, the measures encouraged head teachers to shut the entire school. This was because school closures were <u>excluded</u> from the truancy figures. Instead of a few children missing school this decision deprived every child in the school of a full day of education.

'Targeted truancy' study issues and failure types

Key features, issues, and problem types from this study:

* It was clearly not intended that head teachers close schools as a means of 'improving' their truancy figures. **Using loopholes DB-04, User input misclassification DB-05** and **Unexpected adverse outcomes DB-06**
* Failure to identify the full range of reasons for absence. When snow arrives, it is likely to cause an increase in

unauthorised absences, but not through any fault of either the school or pupils, yet it is treated in the same way (statistically) as truancy. **Incomplete rule definition TF-02** and **Individual and organisational success not aligned TF-08**

- Unbalanced penalty. The 'punishment' for a head teachers shutting the school was clearly regarded as less severe than for 'breaching' the truancy target. **Intense management pressure MF-03, Weak/no link to intended positive outcome TF-06** and **Extreme reward or punishment IF-02**

The four families of problems

The eight case studies demonstrate most of the 33 issues that are causes or symptoms of target, incentive, or management problems. Next, we group them into four families, to make things a bit more orderly. Here are the four groupings...

A. Target Design Failure: Issues with the way in which the targets are designed, indicated with the prefix **TF**.

B. Incentive Design Failure: Problems with the rewards, incentives, or punishments on offer for achieving the target (or not), indicated with the prefix **IF**.

C. Management Dysfunction: Management behaviours that make things worse, shown with the prefix **MF**.

D. Behavioural dysfunction: Weird behaviours that often occur as a result of the other three problem families. We use the prefix **DB** to flag these.

All 33 failure types are listed in the Appendix along with a full explanation and example of each issue.

The ROKET-DS™ Diagnostic

Looking at the failure modes we have identified, it becomes clear that certain issues like to travel in groups. For example 'Winner takes all' incentives can drive 'Law breaking', 'Rule bending or breaking', 'Using loopholes' and other kinds of behavioural dysfunction.

In any busy, complex organisation there are many things going on simultaneously. Some issues will be highly visible, others may be buried and remain undetected. As there are multiple, often intertwined, relationships between these issues, a diagram can really help.

To help make sense of these complex relationships we have developed a schematic called the ROKET-DS™ diagnostic. Here it is...

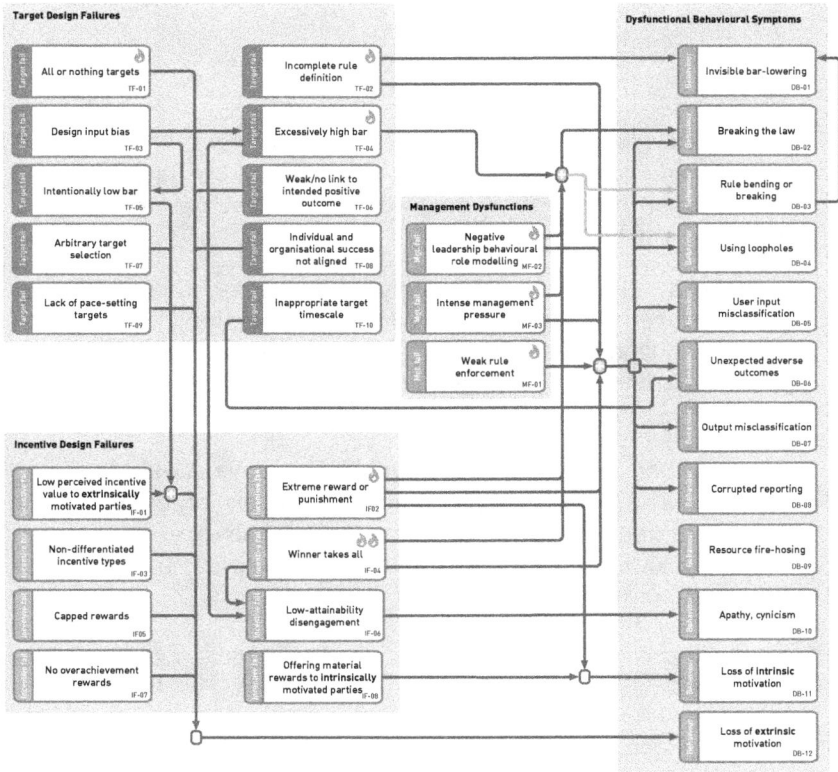

ROKET-DS™ Diagnostic Schematic ©Bernie Smith 2021

You can see all 33 of our common failures identified in our case studies laid out in a structured way along with the plumbing that links them.

The links show how certain failure types are related. You can see how 'Capped rewards', 'No overachievement rewards' or 'Low perceived incentive value' can all lead to 'Loss of extrinsic motivation' (more about motivation types and in particular extrinsic motivation on page 175).

What do the different colour connectors mean?

Note: You can review the colour of the links using your ROKET-DS Diagnostic PDF download.

The dark-grey links represent cause and effect. An incentive which is regarded as unachievable ('Low attainability disengagement' in our diagnostic terminology) will <u>cause</u> 'Loss of intrinsic motivation'.

The red links show actively destructive Dysfunctional Behavioural Symptoms, such as law breaking, corrupted reporting and resource fire-hosing (a full set of definitions can be found in the Appendix, page 255). Put simply, 'the really bad stuff' that people do in a tight spot.

The amber links show actively disruptive Dysfunctional Behavioural Symptoms, 'Rule bending or breaking', and 'Using loopholes'. Put another way these are the 'quite naughty' things that people will do when trying to hit tough targets.

You may be wondering why 'Rule breaking' and 'Using loopholes' have both red and amber links. The link colour is dependent on whether management dysfunctions are involved too. All three management dysfunctions, and a handful of Target and Incentive Design failures, are what are called 'accelerants'. These are things that on their own don't normally cause issues, but can make other behaviours a lot worse. One of the most extreme accelerants is 'Winner takes all'. You only have to look at the world of professional sport, in particular professional cycling, to realise the extreme lengths that people go to to win when it's 'Winner takes all'.

Accelerants are flagged with a little flame icon — think gasoline on a bonfire.

How do we use the ROKET-DS™ Diagnostic?

The ROKET-DS™ Diagnostic can be used in two situations. Firstly....

1. Diagnosing existing target and incentive issues

It's quite common to have a target incentive system that is not performing as expected, which we need to 'fix'. In this situation an accurate diagnosis of all of the issues is essential before we start the repair process. The ROKET-DS™ Diagnostic will help us tease out some of the less obvious problems by using the highly visible issues as a starting point.

Diagnosing existing target and incentive issues is Step 0 of the ROKET-DS™ method, which we will cover in Part 2 of this book. The ROKET-DS™ Diagnostic is the tool we use to do this.

2. Field testing new target and incentive designs for potential problems

One of the major gaps in the SMART method is the lack of 'real world' testing. In Step 7 of our process we will cover a testing process called 'Black-hat testing', where we look for potential problems with our new designs before they are deployed. The ROKET-DS™ Diagnostic is a critical part of that 'black hat testing'.

Part 1: How and why targets and incentives go wrong

Part 2: How to design effective targets (or fix broken ones)

Part 2: How to design effective targets (or fix broken ones)

ROKET-DS

Introducing the ROKET-DS™ method

We have spent time and effort identifying all the different ways in which targets and incentives can go wrong. That's going to prove useful shortly, but to get value from this, we're going to need to create a system for getting things right in the first place and to help us fix existing targets and incentives.

That system is called ROKET-DS™, which stands for 'Results Orientated KPI Effective Target-Design System'. It's not the best name, but it is going to be your new best friend when it comes to navigating your way through the minefield that is target and incentive design.

It is a big method, with up to 15 steps. I make no apology for that. We discovered through our case studies that human behaviour is complex and there are many surprising and unexpected ways in which things can go wrong. A five-step process would be lovely, if it worked. Unfortunately, experience tells us five steps won't cut it here.

There are two distinct elements to the ROKET-DS™ method. The first half is focused on target design — finding that yardstick against which we measure our performance. The second half is the incentive design - thinking about the rewards or punishments that we get for hitting or missing the targets. It is not uncommon to design targets without incentives, or vice versa, so the method is split in two. Part 2 of this book covers target design and Part 3 is on incentive design.

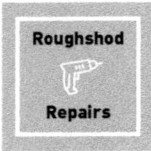

Roughshod Repairs

Like many people, I find things much easier to understand when given an example. To help bring each of the ROKET-DS™ process steps to life, we have a fictional case study — Roughshod Repairs — where we show how the method would be applied in practice. Roughshod Repairs is run by Ruby Roughshod and specialises in managing warranties, repairs, and recalls for consumer electronics manufacturers. As part of the business, they run a call centre with about 100 seats. We've chosen a call centre as it's a measurement-heavy environment that most of us have got some experience of even if it's only as a customer. So, you should have a good intuitive grasp of what they do and also how things can go wrong.

After the theoretical bit of each step, you will find a short section showing how the folks at Roughshod Repairs applied that step to their organisation.

Grow-your-own targets and incentives

For many, the best way to learn is to apply fresh knowledge to their own situation straight away. Each Roughshod case study is followed by a nudge to work on your own targets and incentive design, if you choose to do so whilst you work through this book. The worksheets you will use to do this are called the 'ROKET-DS™ Design Canvases'.

The ROKET-DS™ Design Canvases

I don't have a great memory, middle age isn't helping, and there are a number of steps in our method, so we have created two useful ROKET-DS™ Canvases to make sure you have all the steps at your fingertips. Those canvases are the ROKET-DS™ Target Canvas and the ROKET-DS™ Incentive Canvas.

Both are printable sheets, showing each step of the method, some memory jogging crib notes, and blank space to populate with your answers.

These canvases can be used together, or individually. The printable PDFs can be found in your download pack. They are best printed out on a big sheet of paper (A3/Tabloid or larger) but there is also a much less pretty but more practical Excel version, with all the fields listed in columns and a blank column to populate.

Even though I'm a technology enthusiast, I have found that the paper versions often work out better, particularly for groups, so go for that option if it's at all practical. I often use sticky notes to allow revision and to make it easier for several people to contribute.

Here's what the Target Design Canvas looks like...

ROKET-DS®

Target Design Canvas

Designed by: _____

Target reference: _____ Incentive reference: _____

Date: _____ Version & revision date: _____

0. Identify existing issues
Existing targets and issues?
Side-effects, symptoms & problems?

1. Plan outcome
Intended high-level outcome?
Why is this outcome important?

2. Match KPIs
Which KPIs show if you are moving towards 'Planned outcome'?

3. Identify & engage target owners
Who can influence the Step 2 KPIs?

4. Check owner agency
Do owners have skills, time, resources, authority to move towards the target?

5. Draft target values & rules
Decide on target values
Create 'rules' for achieving targets

6. White-hat test target
What should happen?

7. Black-hat test target
Reverse brainstorm how to hit targets in worst-possible way
Apply **ROKET-DS Diagnostic**

8. Fix problems & re-test
Put in place mitigations to prevent 'worst possible' behaviours to hit targets

9. Record & share targets
How will targets be stored & shared?
How to manage changes & updates?

Now we have introduced the ROKET-DS™ Target Design Canvas, let's get started with our ten-step target design method....

Step 0

Identify existing
issues

Step 0: Identify existing issues

In some situations, you will want to fix an <u>existing</u> target-reward system that is not working properly or is having unintended negative side effects.

We call this 'Step 0' as it's an optional pre-step to the full method. If you are creating your target-reward model from a blank sheet just head straight to Step 1.

What happens in Step 0:

Having a clear understanding of the existing issues is important for two reasons.

Firstly, we need to use the problems and failings of the existing targets and incentives to help us build better ones. For example, if we find that current targets are driving the use of loopholes in the rules, we may need to put more thorough rules in place, perhaps measure a broader range of things or improve policing of the system.

Secondly, we can use our understanding of <u>why</u> and <u>when</u> we have problems with our current system to test our new system — in Steps 7 & 12, 'Black-hat' testing.

To identify our existing problems, we need to...

1. Identify the key stakeholders in the target or reward system you need to fix or improve. A stakeholder is anyone who is involved in either managing, administering, or participating in the target or incentive system.

2. Talk to those stakeholders. Do this in one-to-one conversations or in a group workshop. One-to-one sessions may help individuals 'open up more' (as long as they feel comfortable with their interviewer). Group sessions are particularly useful where you have complex, multi-stage processes, with lots of hand-offs between those stages. The group can often stumble across useful revelations through the workshop process, which would not have been identified otherwise. The ROKET-DS™ Diagnostic is a great tool for prompting discussion. Typically it's best to introduce the group to the tool when they have already had a free-form discussion about the issues and are starting to run out of steam.

3. Make detailed notes about the issues identified. Make sure you know who to go back to if you need clarification.

4. Classify the issues you identified using the ROKET-DS™ Diagnostic.

Classifying problem information in the four 'failure families' and identifying which 'failure types' are present will make things simpler, more thorough, and easier to digest.

Case study example: Roughshod Repairs Call Centre

Roughshod

Repairs

After a very successful marketing campaign, call volumes have steadily increased over the last two years. Their first reaction was to recruit more agents to increase capacity, but Ruby is starting to wonder whether they are as efficient as they could be. To improve agent efficiency Ruby decided to set an 'Average Handling Time, AHT' target for each of the agents coupled with the bonus. Her logic is "The faster we can handle calls, the more calls per agent per hour we can handle, the lower the cost per call and the shorter the average queue time." She sees this as win-win situation: costs will be lower and customers will be happier.

The scheme was introduced under the title 'Project Mercury' and was presented to the call centre staff as a great opportunity for them to boost their wages. If agents hit, or exceeded, their individual AHT targets they could boost their weekly income by as much as 30%. If a team leader's entire team hit their targets, the team leader gets a 50% bonus.

Things seemed to get off to a great start, the 'calls per hour rate' shot up and almost all of the staff hit their bonus targets. A few days after the incentive scheme was introduced Ruby started to get a trickle, then a cascade of emails and phone calls from very unhappy customers. Selected quotes from the customer complaints:

- Your man couldn't get me off the call fast enough! (Rushed calls).
- I was sent on a wild goose chase, being transferred from person to person.
- Your agent just hung up on me (customer call cut-offs).
- I was fobbed off with some excuse that meant I had to call back later with some trivial information.

- I had to call six times and my problem is <u>still</u> not resolved.
- I've had it, I'm going to the press!

Ruby decided to investigate by talking directly to some of the call handlers and their team leaders. After the initial excitement of the bonus scheme had worn off they complained of...

- Feeling like 'Big Brother' is watching them — feeling intense pressure from their team leaders to hit the AHT target
- Not being able to spend the time needed to solve the customers' problems properly, deal with the customers politely, or to build rapport
- Having to deal with very angry customers calling back after being cut off or passed to another team
- Feeling reluctant to work on product helplines where the calls were regarded as 'challenging'
- Not having enough time to write up the call notes
- Agents missing a bonus target due to <u>external</u> factors and receiving nothing
- Team leaders missing their target because of weak or new agents
- Incorrectly marking calls as resolved
- Not understanding where the actual AHT targets came from, or what the figures were based on. In truth, Ruby had just come up with a figure that she thought 'would be a stretch' for the team.

Further research and observation also identified that some agents had discovered that you could 'improve' your 'Average Handling Time' score by switching their status to 'mandatory training' on the system whilst writing up notes or taking a bathroom break, as this time category was excluded from 'available time' in the AHT calculation, so there was one more issue to add to the list:

- Gaming of system status codes to take breaks

Ruby sat down, a little disheartened, after the workshop session and identified each of the ROKET-DS™ Diagnostic failures highlighted during the session...

Target Design Failures

Let's review which of our standard design failure types match the problems that Roughshod Repairs are experiencing. Each problem description is preceded by the issue reference number. You can review the full issue descriptions in the Appendix.

TF-01: All or nothing

The bonus was pass/fail. Every team member had to 'pass' for the supervisor to get their bonus.

TF-02: Incomplete rule definition

Using the wrong call classification codes and not passing customers off to 2nd line were not explicitly against the centre rules.

TF-06: Weak/no link to intended positive outcome

Average handling time did not translate into resolved issues and happy customers.

TF-07: Arbitrary target selection

Ruby had just dreamed up a 'stretch target' without any reference to historic performance or any other kind of benchmark.

TF-08: Individual and organisational success not aligned

An agent could hit the AHT target, but have unhappy customers and unresolved problems.

Management Failures

MF-03: Intense management pressure

As the team leaders needed every agent to hit their AHT target for them to win their 50% bonus, they put intense pressure on their teams to hit their targets 'by any necessary means'.

Incentive Design Failures

IF-05: Capped rewards & IF-07 No over-achievement rewards

The top performing agents knew that they could hit their personal targets pretty easily, so they had little motivation to over-deliver.

IF-06: Low-attainability driven disengagement

The weakest performers in the teams had little chance of hitting their AHT targets. Combined with the supervisor's pressure for everyone to hit their targets (so the team leader could get their bonus) this led to high attrition rates, often losing capable but inexperienced new-starters.

Dysfunctional Behavioural Symptoms

DB-03: Rule bending or breaking

Misclassifying breaks using codes such as 'Mandatory training'. This is specifically forbidden by the Roughshod rulebook.

DB-04: Using loopholes

Some agents were manipulating the staff rota to only work on product helplines with typically quick and easy-to-resolve calls.

DB-05: User input misclassification

Some calls were incorrectly routed to 2nd line if the agents thought they were likely to spoil their AHT.

DB-06: Unexpected adverse outcomes

Using Average Handling Time targets was intended to reduce call wait times, improve customer experience, and lead to greater centre capacity. In practice the opposite happened.

DB-07: Output misclassification

Calls were knowingly misclassified by some agents to make their performance look better.

DB-12: Loss of extrinsic motivation

For those who felt they had no chance of hitting the bonus, typically new starters or team leaders with a weak team member, there was noticeable disengagement.

Nudge: Applying this to your targets

If you have existing targets and incentives that are dysfunctional, document those problems and record them in Box 0 of your ROKET-DS™ Target Design Canvas.

Step 1

Plan outcome

Step 1: Plan outcome

When we set targets we are normally hoping to do more of something, do it faster, or do it better.

When people target or incentivise sales staff, the intent is not to make those sales people richer, but to increase the profit of the business. When a fire brigade has a drive to install free smoke alarms, it's not because they want more space at the fire station by shifting their stock of smoke alarms, rather they have a goal to reduce deaths due to domestic fires.

It is important that we understand the underlying, fundamental reason for setting a target. This deeper objective is going to be our ultimate measure of success. Having an eye on the fundamental goal (or strategic goal, if you like) helps stop us becoming obsessed by lower level outcomes that perhaps don't deliver the expected higher level outcome. Sound a bit mystical? Let me share some concrete examples where this has gone wrong...

- Targeting and funding fire departments according to the number of fire calls seems to make sense. Put out more fires and we are all safer, right?

It turns out that if you do this, it actively disincentivises fire departments from doing fire-prevention work.

And a really personal one...

- In the 1970s and 1980s, in the UK, the state paid dentists to fill children's teeth — presumably with the goal of improving the nation's oral health. As an adult who has never needed a tooth filling but has six from his childhood, I can testify that this approach leads to a mouth full of unnecessary tooth fillings.

Let's take a more business-focused example from the US banking sector. The management of Wells Fargo, a major US bank, decided that cross-selling was the key to business success. On the surface it makes good sense. It costs less to cross-sell a product to an existing customer and customers with multiple products are more likely to be loyal. Wells Fargo, under the leadership of Richard Kovacevich, introduced an incentive scheme for employees to sell at least eight products to each customer, called 'Going for Gr-Eight'. "It was his business model," said a former Norwest executive. "It was a religion. It very much was the culture."[16]

The problem was that the focus on 'Going for Gr-Eight' and cross-selling performance was so intense that staff lost sight of the bigger picture. The gaming and 'widespread illegal practice of secretly opening unauthorized deposit and credit card accounts'[17] that the cross-selling targets drove eventually led to a record-breaking $185 million fine from the Consumer Financial Protection Bureau. Creating accounts for fictitious customers, setting up accounts by forging customers' signatures, and selling products to colleagues impersonating customers will not drive the expected benefits of additional profitability and loyalty. Added to that, these behaviours undermined a major implicit objective of any bank: risk management.

The target of cross-selling 8 products to every existing customer was no longer a means to achieve profitability, it became the end in itself — something called **surrogation**.

To make sure that we don't fall into the trap of losing sight of the bigger picture we need to be very clear about why we are using targets and incentives at all.

From experience there are a handful of fundamental business objectives that come up time and time again:

1. Run a profitable and solvent business
2. A growing business
3. A balanced quality of life
4. A legal and compliant business
5. An innovative business
6. Manage risk

These can usually describe the core strategic objectives of most commercial organisations.

Some organisations have a very specific reason for existence. Often these are 'not for profits' that are trying to change the world in a very specific way. We call these 'mission-based' organisations and include many medical charities, educational charities, or single purpose super-projects (think NASA Moonshot). For mission-based organisations we start with the 'Big 6' but we will need one or two 'custom objectives' as well.

What happens in Step 1

1. Gather and review any vision, mission, or strategy statements in the organisation that are directly relevant to your targets or incentives.

2. Review the Big 6 objectives shown above and identify any that apply to your situation.

3. Note down any 'custom objectives' that show up in your vision, mission, or strategy documents, but are not covered by the Big 6. Word each summary custom objective in straight-forward, descriptive language.

Case study example: Roughshod Repairs Call Centre

Roughshod

Repairs

Ruby decides to have a sit down with some of her trusted senior managers and have a deep think about what it is they are fundamentally trying to achieve.

After a couple of hours of too much coffee and heated debate they confirm that all of the Big 6 objectives apply, though a few of them privately wonder about the commitment to 'A balanced quality of life'.

After even more coffee and discussion, they identify that the call centre can:

Increase **productivity**, giving...

- Faster service, shorter queues
- Reduced cost to serve

...leading to better **profitability**

Maintain (or improve) customer satisfaction, giving...

- Strong industry and customer reputation
- Repeat business

...leading to **growth** and greater **profitability**

It may seem a little unusual to not specifically aim for improved customer satisfaction, but Roughshod is subcontracted by the consumer electronics firms to handle customer calls. There is a customer satisfaction element to the supplier assessment, but beyond a certain level of satisfaction there is no upside for Roughshod. The firms that contract Roughshod are also very cost-focused, so Roughshod need to stay competitively priced to retain existing client contracts and win new ones.

So their planned outcomes are:

Greater **growth** and **profitability** driven by...

A. Increased **productivity**

B. Stable, or improved, **customer satisfaction**

They also decide to base productivity on resolved customer issues rather than simple transaction volumes (number of calls handled etc.).

Practical tips for Step 1

Debating strategic outcomes with a group is a high-risk workshop activity. Strategy means different things to different people and those people often [passionately] believe that their view is correct. It is also common for people to view strategy at wildly different levels, with one person fixated on 'great customer service' and another obsessed by 'the reliability of the intranet'.

The Big 6 can help cut through these problems. As various 'curved ball' strategy suggestions are thrown into the discussion, ask the following questions...

A. Is the stated outcome just a variant of one of the Big 6 outcomes?

B. Is the stated outcome a <u>driver</u> of one, or more, of the Big 6 outcomes?

C. Is the stated outcome a <u>custom objective</u>, so extra to the Big 6?

Every possible option should fit into one of those three categories. Category A is easy, we just use the Big 6 definition, or some fine-tuned version specific to the business we are thinking about.

Anything that falls into Category B will be picked up in the next step of the ROKET-DS™ method — pop it on a sticky note, flip chart, or list and we will get to later.

For Category C, carefully craft a plain-language statement. Examples might include:

- 'Spread ideas' (TED talks)
- 'A world free of multiple sclerosis' (National Multiple Sclerosis Society, US)

- 'Maximise PC market penetration' (Microsoft in the 90s, with their 'A computer on every desk and in every home' ambition)

Using the Big 6 will prevent a group spiralling off into a never-ending cycle of debate and help ensure you actually make it to Step 2.

Nudge: Applying this to your targets

Identify your intended high-level outcomes, along with why they are important, then add them to Box 1 of the ROKET-DS™ Target Design Canvas.

Step 2

Match KPIs

Step 2: Match KPIs

In practice, most meaningful strategic objectives need several indicators to give us a complete picture. A very common design problem is targeting <u>too few</u> measures. Doing this increases the chance of gaming and unexpected bad outcomes.

In our Roughshod Repairs case study, by targeting a single measure — Average Handling Time — all manner of unintended things happened, even when the AHT target was being 'met or exceeded'.

Having a basket of carefully selected targeted KPIs is the foundation of a successful system and an effective way to reduce the chances of dysfunctional behaviours and unexpected outcomes.

What happens in Step 2

At its simplest, Step 2 can be a discussion among the key players where they agree on a handful of KPIs that will give a fair and balanced view of how we are progressing towards our ultimate goal — something like 'Grow the business' or 'Increase profitability'. This more informal approach is best suited to micro and small businesses, where the key team members have a good handle on what makes the business tick. It's not without its risks though, as it is easy to overlook important performance measures without realising it. To make sure this doesn't happen, I'd recommend a more thorough, visual approach: building a KPI Tree.

A KPI Tree is a visual tool that allows us to break down a high level outcome into layers of 'smaller' outcomes, which in turn are measurable. It's always easier to explain using an actual tree.

Let's say we have a personal objective to 'Be healthy'. While this is a vitally important outcome, it is not directly measurable. What we need to do is break it down into smaller outcomes, such as sleeping well, eating well, exercising, and so on.

If we take 'Eating well' as one of those outcomes, again this cannot be measured directly but can be broken down into smaller 'chunks'. One of those chunks is 'Managing number of calories consumed'. By this point we have an outcome that can be directly measured.

Here's the branch of the KPI Tree that we have just discussed.

Strategic		Theme		Tactical		KPI
Be Healthy	—	Eat well	—	Manage calorie intake	—	Calories consumed

Of course we need to repeat this process to get a complete view. If we do this we should end up with something that looks like this:

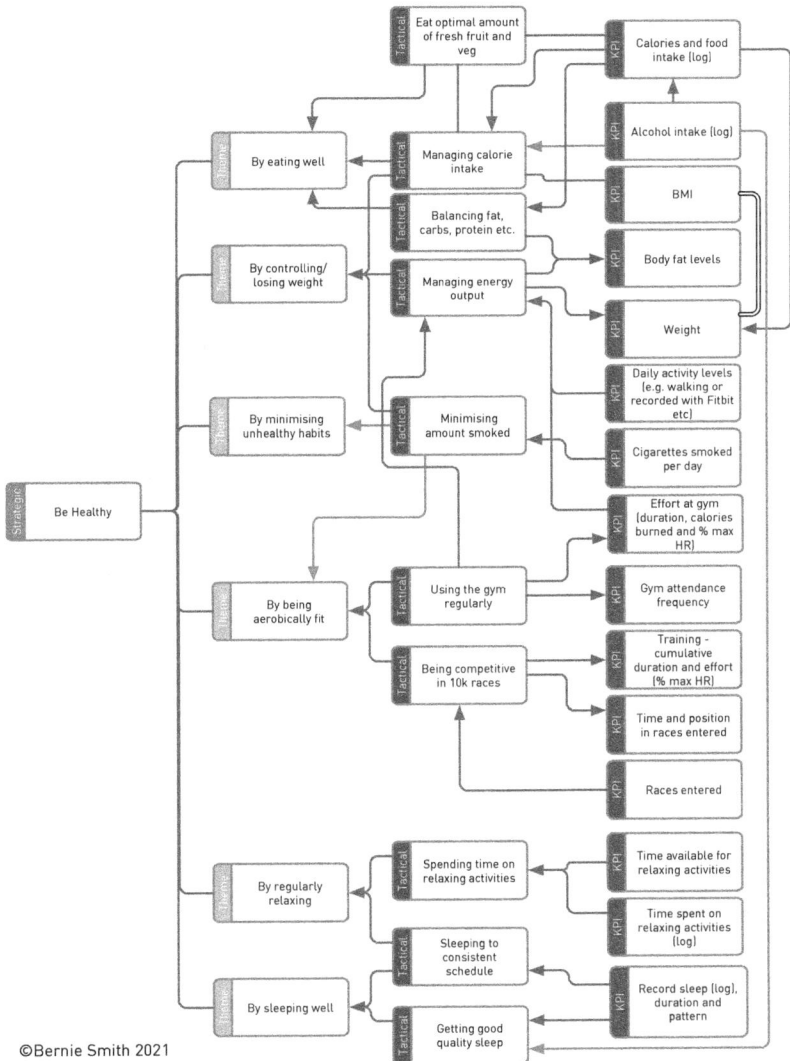

It's important to remember that we are NOT suggesting that you measure all of the things with a 'KPI' marker on their box. These are simply the menu from which we need to choose the final shortlist.

To finalise the list of KPIs, walk through each of the candidate KPIs from the Tree and ask two questions, then score each KPI based on the answer.

KPI review questions:

1. How important is the KPI to our high level outcome? 10 = vital, 0 = no importance
2. How easy is it to measure the KPI? 10 = super easy, no effort, 0 = physically impossible

Next, create a ranking score (Importance Score x Ease of Measurement Score = Ranking Score) and sort the KPIs in descending score order.

The KPIs near the top of the list are both relevant to your objectives and measurable. These then form the raw material for your final discussion about which KPIs to include in your targets and incentive design.

Case study example: Roughshod Repairs Call Centre

Ruby and her team already had a KPI Tree from an earlier project designing their call centre KPIs. They dust off the tree and pull up the relevant section...

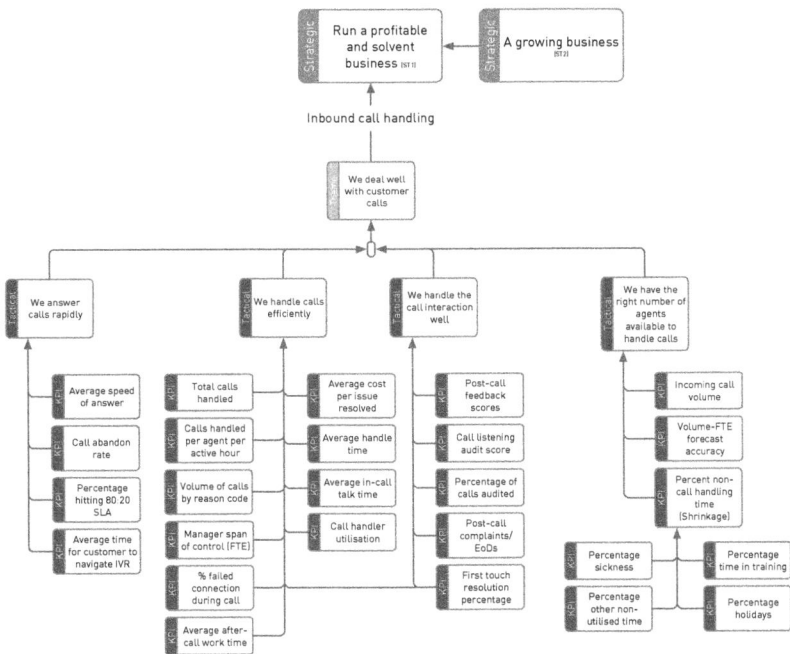

©Bernie Smith 2021

Working through the KPIs on the tree and discussing the importance and ease of measurement of each, they settle on two KPIs:

©Bernie Smith 2021

1. Average Handling Time (seconds per call)

Although the reputation of AHT as a KPI has taken a bit of a hammering, Ruby and her management team still believe it is an important measure as it has a direct impact on:

- Centre capacity
- Staffing requirements
- Call waiting times

It can also be a useful early warning performance indicator for individual agents if it lies significantly outside the normal range.

2. First Touch Resolution (% of calls)

After discussion, everyone agrees that resolving a customer issue on their first call is very important. It has multiple benefits:

- Customers vastly prefer to resolve their issue quickly with a single call.

- There is significant work in recording call notes at the end of an unresolved call and for the next agent to get up to speed in the follow-up call. This also leads to mistakes and frustration during the handover. Customers hate it too.

- It reduces the amount of 'failure demand' — extra calls generated by unresolved issues requiring follow-up by the customer.

Practical tips for Step 2

If you want to find out more about KPI Trees head to the Building KPI tree page on our website (https:// madetomeasurekpis.com/building-kpi-tree/).

Nudge: Applying this to your targets

Identify the KPIs that will show if you are moving towards the 'Planned outcome' of Step 1, then add those KPIs to Box 2 of the ROKET-DS™ Target Design Canvas.

Part 2: How to design effective targets (or fix broken ones)

Step 3

Identify & engage
target owners

Step 3: Identify and engage target owners

Knowing who you need to talk to, gain approval from, or keep updated is central to implementing successful targets and incentives. Many implementation projects fail because of political or communication problems.

Because organisations are complex structures and the people within them are often anxious and busy, the 'Engagement' step is one of the easiest steps to mess up.

In this step we identify everyone who can influence the KPIs that we identified in the previous 'Match KPIs' step, how we will communicate with them, and what message we will be sharing.

After we have identified who to talk to, we will also need to plan how we are going to talk to them.

What happens in Step 3

The simple, smaller business approach to Step 3

For micro and small businesses, at its simplest, this step involves...

A. Making a list of who needs to be involved

B. Working out the depth and type of involvement needed from each person in the process

C. Holding a workshop, perhaps a series of one-to-ones or some combination of the two to introduce the nominated team members to the target and incentive design process, and their role in it.

The larger, more corporate approach to Step 3

Larger organisations are normally more complex, more formal, and more political than smaller ones. Although we essentially follow the same three steps listed for a small business, we need an approach with more detail, structure, and paperwork.

We use a **stakeholder review** to produce a list of names, which we then group based on the type of influence they have on the KPIs we are targeting and create a tailored engagement plan for each stakeholder group. Breaking this down, we have:

1. Identify stakeholders

2. Segment the stakeholders list

3. Put together a simple plan for how you will engage with the stakeholder groups

i. Identify stakeholders

Firstly we identify who is involved, affected, or useful in the target and incentive design process. The catch-all term for these people is 'stakeholder'. Whilst working out who to talk to is usually straightforward in a small organisation, it can become brain-meltingly complex in a multinational.

Our aim is to not only include those who have <u>direct influence</u> over the targeted KPIs but those who have <u>control</u> over resources and systems that have an impact on the performance those KPIs report on. For example, IT services, technical resources, perhaps contractors or specialists who support the processes. Don't forget third-party processing or service providers who may also influence performance results as it may be sensible to include them in the design process too.

The final group of stakeholders we need to consider are **enablers**. These are team members who are not directly involved but may have a significant indirect impact on our targeted performance. This type of stakeholder might include people from quality management, human resources, finance department, training team, or the people who enforce rules in the system — 'policemen and policewomen' of the organisation. We will often need to include this group where they influence the ability of our primary target owners to hit their targets.

Developing the stakeholder list is best done using a spreadsheet so we can sort and group the list (check out the download pack for a simple template to make this super easy).

Be sure to capture:

- The stakeholder name
- Their role

Tip: Use the stakeholder <u>role description</u> to identify stakeholders you don't know personally

The role type can be helpful if you know one or two people in a role, but do not know the names of other, equally relevant team members who should be included. For example, at Roughshod, if we knew that Rachael Reeves is a shift supervisor that we should involve, that's a prompt to identify any other shift supervisors that we may need to talk with.

ii. Segment the stakeholders list

We divide up the list to develop a set of communications plans that are appropriate to each segmented group. You will use a very different communications approach with your CEO versus an update session with a 3rd party IT supplier.

In the column on the righthand side include each stakeholder's name, record their role type and the type of stakeholder they are.

Typical stakeholder segmentation categories:

- Target recipient
- Target recipient's manager (and chain of command)
- Support provider (e.g. IT team)
- Third-party provider (e.g., off-site mail processing provider)
- Enabler (e.g. training team)

Optional: Including stakeholder contact details in your segmentation can make executing the communication plan a bit slicker, particularly in large and complex organisations.

Creating the stakeholder list will enable you to easily sort it by each column, making our next step — communications planning — nice and simple.

iii. Put together a simple plan for how you will communicate and engage with the stakeholder groups

The sophistication of the communications plan will depend on a number of factors. Political sensitivity, number of people affected, the degree of change and complexity in the implementation will all play a part. We have included a set of checklists in the Appendix, borrowed from one of my earlier books, KPI Checklists, to help you create your communications plan.

Case study example: Roughshod Repairs Call Centre

Roughshod Repairs is not a complex organisation. Ruby and her team went through this process and identified the following stakeholder groups...

Project team — the individuals directly involved in the development of the targets and incentives

Agents — they're absolutely crucial and are front and centre of this

Team leaders — many of whom are quality assessors, so they will listen in on calls and will assess their quality

Operations managers play a role because they determine things like shared tooling in conjunction with the resource managers

Customers — here we're talking about the customers of the results

Senior managers — the group that are ultimately accountable for Roughshod's performance

Technical team who keep the system up and running and delivering smoothly

Training team who help agents up-skill and improve their ability to handle the calls compliantly so they end up with happy customers and resolve issues as smoothly and swiftly as possible.

Their communication plan is split into four phases and looks like this:

Project launch
Stakeholders:

- Everyone — face to face

Ruby will do a short section in the monthly 'Centre update' session, sharing the intent and plan for the target and incentive development. She will also prepare an FAQ (frequently asked questions) document for follow-up sessions between the team leaders and agents. The purpose of those sessions is to handle any anxieties or objections.

Target and Incentive development
Stakeholders:

- Project team, Senior managers — face to face
- Everyone — email

A team will be put together for designing and building the targets and incentives. They will report to the board on a weekly basis in a 20 minute face-to-face discussion and write a weekly update email for the whole centre team.

Target launch
Stakeholders:

- Project team, Operations Managers, Team Leaders — face-to-face two-hour workshop
- Agents, Customers, Technical team, Training team — cascade meetings

Once the targets and incentives are designed, all Team Leaders will go through a two-hour workshop on how the targets and incentives were designed, what issues there may be, and expected questions and anxieties. They will then brief their teams through the daily team cascade, face to face.

Post-launch Q&A

Stakeholders:

- Agents, Team Leaders — face-to-face one-to-ones
- Project team, Team Leaders — feedback session from one-to-ones

After the first round of targets and incentive results, the team leaders will have one-to-ones with each of their team members to identify their comfort level and any concerns and issues they may have. These will then be fed back, anonymously, to the development team in a meeting with the Team Leaders.

Nudge: Applying this to your targets

Now is the time to record the names of the team members you need to be involved in the target design, adding them to Box 3 of the ROKET-DS™ Target Design Canvas.

Step 4

Check owner agency

Step 4: Check owner agency

It does not matter how motivated a person is if they are not able to meaningfully influence the thing they are targeted to achieve. This problem is best summarised by this quote from The Telegraph's obituary of Eric Hall, record promoter turned football agent...

> *He was able to make deals despite confessing that he knew little about football. Asked to negotiate Dave Beasant's move from Wimbledon to Newcastle, he came out of the meeting with the club and proudly told the player that he had got him a bonus of £100,000 if he scored 10 goals. Beasant informed Hall that he was a goalkeeper.*

Daily Telegraph, Wednesday 18th November 2020

Clearly a bonus of £100,000 is attractive, but not particularly achievable if you are the goalkeeper.

We call this ability to hit the target 'agency'. It's a combination of factors that need to be in place in order to give them a fighting chance of achieving the outcome that we're looking for.

It is important to remember that we are not talking about making it <u>easy</u>, but making sure they have at least a fighting chance of hitting the targets we set.

What happens in Step 4:

In this step we aim to answer the question: "Can the person/ team you are targeting realistically influence, in the desired way, the thing that you are targeting them with changing?"

We can break this down into smaller questions by asking, "If properly motivated, does this person/team have the...

- Skills
- Time
- Authority
- Resources

...to positively influence the thing we want to target?"

These four points are the 'Ingredients of Agency' and form the acronym **STAR**, to make them a little easier to remember.

If the answer to all of these questions is 'yes', then we are all set and ready to move on to Step 5. If the answer to any of those bullet points is 'no' then you have two sensible options and one very dangerous one:

1. Check that you are applying targets to the correct person/team within the organisation. Are there others who have better agency to improve the outcome you are targeting?
2. If you are sure you are targeting the right person/ team then you will need to fix or improve each of the

problematic 'Ingredients of Agency'. This might involve providing additional tools, skills training, or extra resources.

3. Compensate for the lack of agency by making the reward irresistible. This is highly dangerous and will normally result in failure at high human cost with possible legal repercussions.

If someone offered me £1 million to jump, unassisted, three metres in the air, it really doesn't matter what the sum of money is, I just couldn't do it without cheating. A situation where we pile on more reward to overcome a lack of agency is incredibly dangerous and will normally result in failure and high human costs, possibly with legal repercussions. People put in this situation are highly prone to stress-related illness, cheating, and illegal behaviour.

This check is very important to make sure that we're not setting people up for failure, rule breaking, or illegal behaviour.

Case study example: Roughshod Repairs Call Centre

Roughshod Repairs

Ruby and her managers review whether their agents have agency over the two selected KPIs from Step 2. They discuss whether agents have the...

- Skills
- Time
- Authority
- Resources

...to positively influence 'Average Handling Time' and 'First Touch Resolution'.

Roughshod STAR review: Average Handling Time

Ruby and her managers agree that agents <u>do</u> have the necessary authority and resources to influence AHT positively.

Skills: Roughshod Repairs, like most call centres, has a skills management programme in place and a training team. So, whilst at any given time not all agents are <u>fully</u> skilled because of team churn, there are processes and methods in place for identifying skills shortfalls, training people up, and tracking skills. So Ruby and her team are pretty confident that most of the fully trained team members have full agency for Average Handling Time.

Time: Do agents have enough time? This is an interesting question, as the KPI itself is a measure of how much time we spend on each call, on average. If we set the handling time target too aggressively, we will create a situation in which agents do not have enough time. We will need to consider how long is 'long enough' to handle a call well when we come to the target setting stage, the next step.

Authority: If agents do not have the necessary authority they will pass the case to their supervisor. This will 'stop the clock', so will not have an adverse impact on their AHT (this is an issue, as it can drive the wrong behaviour in some situations). So, from the point of view of improving AHT, the agents have the authority they need.

Resources: Ruby believes that agents have the right resources in about 98% of calls handled. There is a small subset where they don't have what they need, and the call will have to be passed off to second line. Again this will 'stop the clock' so the agent is not penalised for not having the correct resources.

Roughshod STAR review: First Touch Resolution

Skills: Looking at the agent skills for First Touch Resolution they come to a similar conclusion to AHT, that is... all of the fully qualified staff should have the necessary skills. In practice this does not mean that every qualified agent can resolve every call on first touch, as about 10-20% of the calls are too complex to do this, but this is the basis on which the centre is designed.

Time: Currently, agents are under pressure to close calls as quickly as possible. With the new targets, this will change. There is going to be a balance between Average Handling Time and First Touch Resolution and we're going to review the AHT targets with an eye to resolving problems. So, it's not going to be 'as fast as possible', it's going to be asking, "Can we deal with the calls in the time it should take?"

Authority: In around 84% of calls handled, agents do have the necessary authority to do what's required, and again, a small proportion need to be passed off to second line support to resolve them.

Resources: Ruby believes that agents have the right resources in about 96% of calls handled. There is a small subset where they don't have what they need, and that will have to be passed off to second line.

By the end of the exercise, Ruby and her team agree that, for fully qualified agents, they do have the necessary skills, time, authority, and resources, in the majority of cases as long as the AHT targets set are not overly aggressive.

Nudge: Applying this to your targets

Having identified your target owners in Step 3, review whether those owners have full agency. Do the target owners have the skills, time, authority, and resources needed to move towards the target? Record your answers in Box 4 of the ROKET-DS™ Target Design Canvas.

Step 5

**Draft target
values & rules**

Step 5: Set draft target values

This is the step where we have our first attempt to set the actual target values and rules for the KPIs that we selected in Step 2.

It is tempting to offer generous rewards to our very best performers who manage to reach our demanding stretch targets, a kind of 'school prize day' for our organisation. It makes sense because many of us are used to this kind of reward system.

If we take a step back and think about what we are really trying to achieve, just targeting and rewarding 'the best of the best' doesn't necessarily make sense. Superstar performers do outperform 'average' performers in a one-to-one comparison, but there are always far more 'average' performers in an organisation than superstars, so it makes no sense to ignore the average performers.

To get the biggest organisational benefit, we should be aiming to motivate every single individual in the organisation to deliver the very best performance 'stretch' that they can.

Ideally, this involves personalised targets. In practice this can be logistically overwhelming, so tiered targets can be a sensible compromise.

To create those tiered targets, we need a structured workshop session. In that session we need to think about:

A. Historic performance levels

B. Any changes in 'agency' that may affect the target compliance rate (e.g., new systems, improved training, or market shifts)

C. The 'influence range' of our targets and target tiers

D. The impact of target achievement

E. The expected proportion of the target owners that will hit the target (target compliance rate)

What happens in Step 5

Let's look at the workshop approach and each of these steps in more detail.

Setting up a target design workshop

The biggest risk of a target design workshop is that it loses touch with facts, figures, and structure. Without good quality reference information, target design can easily become loud and wild 'horse trading'. The best way to avoid this is to have good quality data to hand, a clear set of goals for each session, and strong facilitation. It also makes sense to build some time in between sessions to allow everyone to 'sleep on it'.

The other risk is slipping into a discussion of the size and shape of incentives. Remember, we will be covering this in Part 3 of the ROKET-DS™ method, so don't get pulled into this emotional minefield ahead of the plan.

In the target design workshop we will review:

Historic performance levels

Historic performance can tell us a number of things such as:

- What average level of performance can we expect to achieve?

This is a key figure for calculating our performance 'baseline' and the value of any performance improvement we see.

- What range of performance do we see in our population (e.g., sales people, call agents etc.)?

We need to understand this if we want to set up multiple 'tiers' of targets.

- What peaks in performance do we see?

This gives us a glimpse of 'what is possible'. It is important to understand context and circumstance before drawing too many conclusions, but this figure is one of the best responses to a tough target being described as 'impossible'.

Any changes in <u>agency</u> that may affect the target compliance rate (e.g., new systems, improved training, or market shifts)

Historic performance figures are a useful start point, but it is important to factor-in other events that may naturally push those figures up (or down) aside from any targets we set. Examples include:

- New IT systems
- Process automation (RPA etc.)
- New rules or regulations
- Process improvements
- Changes in team or ownership, particularly where they affect skill levels

- Change in product/case/work mix

Where we expect a change, it is necessary to estimate the impact of that change, so we can scale or adjust historic performance figures to take account of this. If possible, it's best to do some real-world testing, even if it's only a rough approximation.

The 'influence range' of our targets and target tiers

If I can normally run a mile in ten minutes and I was offered an attractive reward for running that mile in nine minutes thirty seconds, that is a sensible stretch target which may well motivate me. If I, as an overweight middle-aged writer, was offered a generous reward for running a 4:30 mile, it would have no motivating effect as it is way out of my range of potential performance. Clearly there is a boundary, or zone, past which a target ceases to have a motivating effect. When debating target values, it is up to the group to try and estimate where those boundaries or zones lie and how to tier targets to make sure that the whole team remains motivated.

The impact of target achievement

The purpose of a target is always to deliver an improved, or less negative, outcome. Targets carry a practical and economic overhead, so we need to balance the effort and cost with the benefits we expect. Put simply: is the effort worth the reward? We need to check this before we go too far down the target design process.

If the benefit does not justify the cost and effort, then we could be focusing on the wrong performance measure or may have messed up our initial potential-benefit calculations.

The percentage of the target owners who will hit the target (target compliance rate)

In economics there is a well-known effect called 'price elasticity', where demand is affected by price, and as a result there is an optimum price to maximise profit. There is a similar curve for targets.

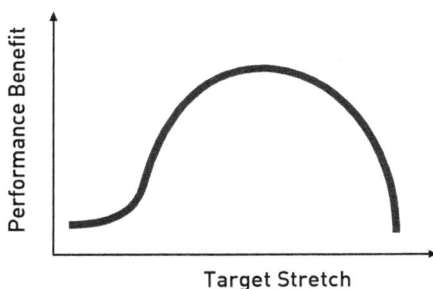

In this curve we see that, up to a point, increased stretch will deliver greater overall benefit. Past that point, the benefit of achieving that extra performance is more than offset by the reduced population that are motivated or able to hit that tougher target.

Going 10x on your targets?

If you have just read Grant Cardone's 10x you might well feel a super demanding target is the way to go. Think carefully before you do this. Yes, very aggressive targets will motive some of your team, but they may also alienate a segment who could still have delivered a valuable boost to the team's performance, but don't have the confidence or drive to strive for a 10x target. If few, or none of the team are motivated by it, then the practical benefits fall far below potential. If you do go down the 10x route, you must use tiered targets to avoid missing out on the benefits that the 'journeyman' team members can bring to the table.

Bigger organisations, more complexity

For larger, more complex organisations answering these questions may also involve some 'what-if modelling' in a spreadsheet. The organisational impact can be forecast using this relationship:

Sum of [(**benefit impact** [per % point]) x (**target-induced performance lift** [%age])]

You may need to do some testing and experimentation to understand the relationship between target values and performance uplift.

Some extra thoughts on setting target values

Anyone who has had to negotiate targets in the real world knows that there are some common challenges that often come up during those discussions.

Struggling to set target tiers

Sometimes it can be tough to start putting figures to each of your target tiers. If you find yourself in this situation, posing the question, "What level of performance would just be plain embarrassing?" can often help to get things started.

You can extend this approach by asking how each person would feel sharing a range of specific performance figures with a peer or friend in the sector. Their emotional response will give a good gauge of their perception of the performance level for a given result.

Here are some example emotional responses and how they might map to performance levels:

- Embarrassment — unacceptable performance

- Discomfort — poor performance
- Indifference — middle-of-the road performance
- Joy — above average performance
- Can't wait to tell everyone! — outstanding performance

Obviously the exact emotions and achievement levels vary, but the idea of connecting results with emotions can help bring things to life and 'unstick' the conversation.

Comparing performance with other players: Benchmarking

An entire industry has sprung up around benchmarking, the process by which you compare your performance with similar organisations to yours. It's a seductively simple idea, but it is fraught with risk. It's not uncommon to have two KPIs with the same name but different definitions within the same business. This problem becomes more acute across separate organisations, so be very cautious about placing too much importance on comparisons.

The safest situation in which to use competitor benchmarking is when you can verify their performance yourself. Examples include:

- Price
- Delivery time
- Stock levels
- Call answer time

Target setting 'sandbagging'

Sandbagging is the process where you ask for too much (or deliberately offer too little), knowing that you will be then be forced to 'concede' some extra target performance by your boss.

A departmental head might know that 75% efficiency is achievable, but promise 65% knowing that her boss has a habit of upping targets by 5-10% to make them 'stretch'. By lowering the promise to 65% she has already factored that stretch requirement in, so it is no longer a genuine stretch.

The tendency to sandbag and haggle varies by organisation, individual, and culture, but there are certain things that make it more likely:

- Severe punishment or consequences for failure, including humiliation, legal action, or career blight
- A risk-averse personality
- An intelligent player who can see that long-term improvement is rewarded and wants to pace the delivery rate of that improvement

There is no magic wand for dealing with sandbagging, though historic data is one of your strongest tools. Picking a particularly strong performance period can often give you some hard evidence of what's possible and can be hard to argue with, just be mindful of any genuinely exceptional circumstances surrounding that peak performance.

Case study example: Roughshod Repairs Call Centre

Roughshod

Repairs

Sticking to the method, the Roughshod team pull together a group to plan the specific values of the targets for the **Average Handling Time** and **First Touch Resolution** KPIs they chose earlier.

They pull out the objectives from Step 1 and remind themselves of their goal.

Greater **growth** and **profitability** driven by:

A.   Increased **productivity**

B.   Stable, or improved **customer satisfaction**

Analysing the figures, Ruby has calculated that a 12% increase in productivity (cases resolved and closed by agents) will comfortably make Roughshod the lowest priced provider out of the three big players in this market space. Customer satisfaction rates are currently running at 78%, comfortably above their contractual requirement of 70+%.

Ruby sets the group the challenge of answering five questions:

1.   What target values align with the planned outcome?

2.   What Average Handling Time figure would deliver a 12% improvement in productivity?

For both Average Handling Time and First Touch Resolution, what would...

3.   'Acceptable' performance look like?

4.   'Good' performance look like?

5.   'Outstanding' performance be?

The team agrees that they will split the targets into three performance levels and agrees beforehand the proportions of the team that will achieve each of the higher two levels.

They decide the bottom tier will be named 'solid' — this is the minimum standard that they need to offer to be compliant and to offer a sustainable service to remain 'in business'.

The next level up will be 'good' — this is the service standard that we expect the top third or so of our agents to be able to achieve on a regular basis, so good but not necessarily superstars.

The top tier is 'legendary' — this is the standard that we expect the top 2% of agents to achieve on a regular basis for both Average Handling Time and First Touch Resolution.

Next, Ruby reviews historic performance and looks at the data, setting the target values to reflect those past performance figures for the top two levels: the performance aspirations for the business.

Here are the levels they set:

KPI	Level 1: Solid	Level 2: Good	Level 3: Legendary
First Touch Resolution	→ 65%	→ 75%	→ 80%
Average Handling Time	← 240 seconds	← 220 seconds	← 210 seconds

Wrapping up their workshop, they now have the first draft of their target figures. The next two steps are about testing these targets for robustness.

Nudge: Applying this to your targets

Give your target values and rules some thought and discussion, then record them in Box 5 of the ROKET-DS™ Target Design Canvas.

Part 2: How to design effective targets (or fix broken ones)

Step 6

White hat test
targets

Step 6: Targets white hat testing

In 1903, a short Western movie called 'The Great Train Robbery' set a convention that lasted for over 40 years. The good guys wore white hats, and the bad guys wore black hats. In our ROKET-DS™ method, we use the same terminology to describe our two target testing approaches.

What happens in Step 6:

Our first testing step is 'white hat testing'. In this step, we ask one simple question:

What should happen when people display the behaviours we expect and encourage in the context of targets?

In this step we are not trying to anticipate any problems or issues, we just walk through the expected behaviour. This does not mean we always assume an ideal outcome, just that our system of targets functions according to the rules and people behave in the way we anticipated when building the initial targets.

White hat testing is normally uneventful, just a case of walking through the thought process and logic that we used in the earlier steps. There are typically few surprises. However, it is an important precursor for the following step, black hat testing.

Case study example: Roughshod Repairs Call Centre

Let's take a look at Roughshod Repairs and their white hat testing and see what it looked like.

Ruby and her managers ask the question: "What should happen when people display the behaviours we expect and encourage?" In an ideal world, our agents deal with calls swiftly, they resolve the customer's problem on first touch wherever possible, and they stay polite and legally compliant all the way through every single call. By the end of the call the customer is delighted by their experience interacting with the Roughshod agent.

We acknowledge that, even in an ideal world, a small percentage of calls will be outside the capability of the frontline agents, so these get passed smoothly and seamlessly to second line support where our customer's issues are resolved, swiftly, politely, and legally compliantly by the appropriate specialist agent.

White hat testing is just the start

Most people are excellent game players, and humans have evolved to make the best of any situation. This applies to KPIs and targets too. And as anyone who's played any kind of board game knows, even the most morally upright player will, when appropriately motivated, challenge, bend, stretch, and even break the rules in an attempt to win. And this is the kind of behaviour we will be trying to flush out in our next step, 'black hat testing'.

Nudge: Applying this to your targets

Time to consider how your targets <u>should</u> work by walking through the inputs and outputs of each target. Record the key points of the walk-through in Box 6 of the ROKET-DS™ Target Design Canvas.

Step 7

Black hat test
targets

Step 7: Targets black hat testing

This step is all about spotting real world, unintended responses to our draft targets before we go live and before we discover those issues in the worst possible way.

We call this non-textbook type of behaviour 'black hat testing'.

What do black hat behaviours look like in practice? Here are three black hat behaviours from a real [anonymous] US sales organisation, to give you a flavour:

- Salespeople ship orders ahead of schedule to hit the current monthly targets.

- Opening bad-credit accounts, knowing the customers would not actually pay the invoice, as the sales team know they are paid on gross profit based on invoicing, not on paid invoices.

- Hiding inventory from other sales teams by temporarily shipping stock 'out of state' by courier. When other sales teams asked for stock, they could honestly tell other divisions that there was no stock in state. However, when their customers needed new inventory, the stock would magically reappear in the state.

These are just examples, but whatever industry you work in, you are probably already familiar with some of dirty tricks people play in order to hit their targets.

In the worlds of military and cyber security, there's a commonly used method for testing your strategy and defences for this kind of behaviour: 'Red Teaming'. Members of the 'friendly' team will take the role of the adversary, becoming the 'red team', and will try and defeat or penetrate your defensive position. The red team is free to use <u>any</u> trick, tool, or tactic to try and defeat the blue team.

This approach can help team members break out of the mental constraints that may stop them spotting weaknesses in existing rules, systems, and processes.

The US army regularly use Red Teaming and describe it as:

Structured, iterative process executed by trained, educated and practiced team members that provides commanders with an independent capability to continuously challenge plans, operations, concepts, organisations and capabilities in the context of the operational environment and from our partners' and adversaries' perspectives.

Black hat testing is a powerful way of avoiding embarrassing unintended outcomes, but also helps us develop a set of robust rules for <u>enforcement</u> of our targets, as we will have a much better idea of the loopholes, cheats, and shortcuts people might use to hit their targets.

What happens in Step 7

The way to think of this step is 'game-proofing' our targets. The good news is that we have two powerful weapons to help us do this: reverse brainstorming and the ROKET-DS™ Diagnostic.

First, let's look at reverse brainstorming:

How reverse brainstorming works

The approach is based on a very simple idea, asking the people affected by the new targets and incentives, "How could the 'right' result be achieved in the stupidest possible way?"

It sounds so simple, you would think there's no possible way it would work. From experience it does work, generally very well.

Running a reverse brainstorming workshop, a step by step guide

A. Identify a handful of people who are closely involved in the day-to-day business of whatever you are interested in improving. Having identified our stakeholders in Step 3, this should be quick and straightforward.

B. Set up a 30–45 minute informal workshop in a quiet room with a flip chart.

C. Make sure the person running the session is not seen as having a bias towards the activity you are looking to reverse brainstorm — i.e. It's not their manager(s) that are trying to implement the 'thing' that you want to reverse brainstorm.

D. Explain the result that is being worked towards, e.g., shorter wait times for email banking query responses.

E. CRITICAL POINT: Make sure the participants in the workshop feel completely safe expressing honest opinions. They must feel that there will be no negative consequences from being completely open and honest. If the group feel they have to be on their best behaviour, this will not work. If you have concerns about using an internal staff member, consider using an external facilitator.

F. Explain the purpose of the workshop and how reverse brainstorming works.

G. Explain the proposed KPIs, targets (for Step 7), incentives (for Step 12), rules, and intended outcomes.

H. Ask the group: "How could the 'right' target/incentive result be achieved in the stupidest possible way?"

I. Use a flip chart, with a vertical line down the middle, and write the 'Stupid' actions in the left-hand column. Real-life examples that have come up in workshops include:

» Booking £186m of bad debt in the wrong category on a balance sheet because 'the board don't look at that category'.

» Not cleaning up a production line during a shift, as that time will be 'lost time' in their efficiency figures. If they leave it, the next shift team have to clear up and will take the performance hit.

» When bonuses are dependent on a 'Six Sigma Quality Score' derived from grading an agent's individual work, asking a friend to score their work, and vice versa, to ensure that both hit their 'bonus scores'.

J. When you have reached the natural end of the 'Stupid' brainstorm, it's time to think about how we can prevent 'Stupid' from happening.

K. In the right-hand column, write ideas for preventing 'Stupid' next to each of the potential target problems the group have identified. Sometimes the solution will involve extra metrics, other times it will be new or refined target rules.

The approach works well because people are generally better at figuring out how things will go <u>wrong</u> rather than how they will go right. Reverse brainstorming taps into that common human ability to spot 'what is broken' and turns it on its head. It's time to harness your team's 'inner pessimist'.

ROKET-DS™ Diagnostic

If you think back to our case studies in Part 1, we distilled the common issues that appear time and time again into a map, showing the 33 identified issues and the relationships between them. This map is called the ROKET-DS™ Diagnostic and is a powerful tool to support our reverse brainstorming conversation.

It is best used after the initial reverse brainstorm. Once the initial flush of team ideas has been discussed and recorded, the ROKET-DS™ Diagnostic can be used to prompt further discussion.

For example, if we identified this issue:

When bonuses are dependent on a 'Six Sigma Quality Score' derived from grading an agent's individual work, asking a friend to score their work, and vice versa, to ensure that both hit their bonus scores.

This problem would fit into these categories:

- Invisible bar lowering (DB-01)
- Rule bending or rule breaking (DB-03)
- Corrupted reporting (DB-08)
- Output misclassification (DB-07)

These boxes are linked to others, and it would be worth exploring with the team whether the following issue types may also be relevant:

- Incomplete rule definition (TF-02)
- Excessively high bar (TF-04)
- Extreme reward or punishment (IF-02)
- Winner takes all (IF-04)
- Weak rule enforcement (MF-01)
- Negative leadership behavioural role modelling (MF-02)
- Intense management pressure (MF-03)

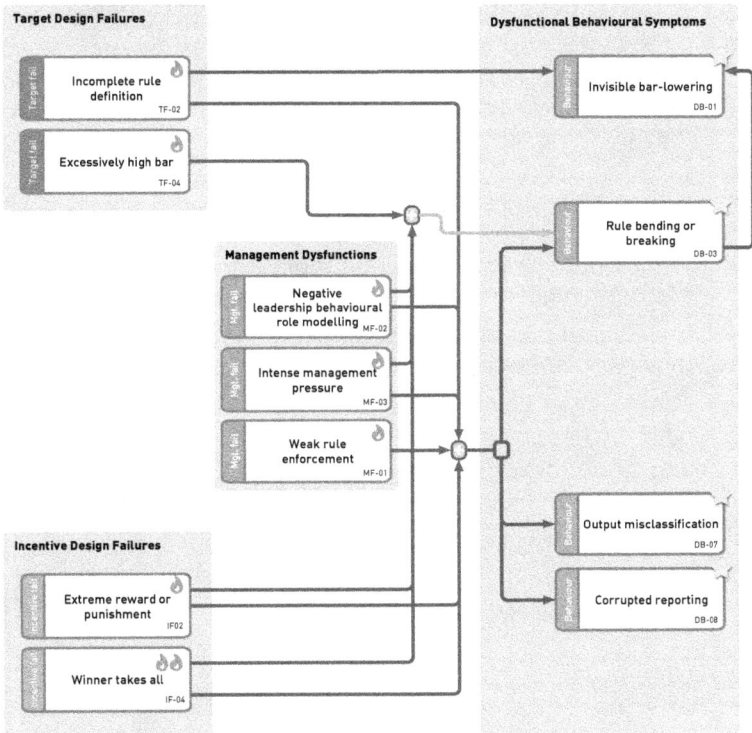

'Six Sigma Quality Score' example ROKET-DS™ Diagnostic

GAMED Design Checklists

The final set of tools that can help us with our 'black hat testing' are the GAMED Design Checklists (included in the Appendix). These are a series of checklists with practical questions to help you examine various aspects of the business that maybe aren't immediately obvious, particularly if you're focusing on the operational side of things, so there are plenty of questions around financial and operational risk.

For example, looking at financial risk:

- What happens in the most extreme financial cases?
- What is the cost and operational impact of the most likely, or most extreme outcomes resulting from hitting the targets we set? e.g., Will our star performer retire if they hit their targets?

Then, we talk about reputational and legal risks:

- What would be the impact on morale from the most extreme successes and failures?
- How would our most extreme outcomes be perceived if they were splashed across a newspaper?
- Legal risk — have we done a legal risk assessment?

Thinking back to our opening story involving emissions, VW Audi, and the EPA, it seems unlikely that these questions were discussed during VW Audi's initial decision-making process.

Case study example: Roughshod Repairs Call Centre

Roughshod

Repairs

In Roughshod Repairs, Ruby decides to call in an external facilitator to run the black hat workshop, Roger Reckless.

Roger focuses on the two KPIs that we came up with in our first pass on target setting:

Average Handling Time and **First Touch Resolution**

He asks the group how an agent could achieve a 'good' performance on both in a way that messes up other, non-targeted KPIs.

The group came up with a number of potential issues:

1. Rushing customer interaction

If we focus solely on Average Handling Time and First Touch Resolution, customer interaction quality could worsen. It's perfectly possible to deal with the call quickly and effectively but still have a customer that feels rushed or feels that the agent has been rude in some way.

2. Cutting corners

The group also pointed out that there are certain classes of call that are impossible to deal with properly within the target Average Handling Time period.

Roger then introduces the ROKET-DS™ Diagnostic. Having already identified that a single Average Handling Time target will be too short for certain types of call, the group then agreed agents would try to 'recover time' by:

- Skipping the legally required in-call disclaimers (Breaking the law DB-02)

- Cutting sections out of the mandatory call scripts (Rule breaking DB-03)
- Rushing call wrap-up to save time
- Passing calls to second line, when the call is a complex one, just to 'stop the AHT clock' (Output Misclassification DB-07)

3. Longer call waits

If we spend our time focusing particularly on First Touch Resolution, we may find that the calls get longer and as a result customer queue times increase.

In the next step, we will look at our options for managing or eliminating these potential issues.

Nudge: Applying this to your targets

It's time to think about how your targets will perform in the real world. Use reverse brainstorming and the ROKET-DS™ Diagnostic to work out the worst possible outcomes and log those results in Box 7 of the ROKET-DS™ Target Design Canvas.

Step 8

Fix problems
& re-test

Step 8: Fix Problems & re-test

In the previous step, Black Hat Testing, we flushed out problems and unintended consequences before launch, to avoid discovering them the hard way.

Once we have uncovered potential issues, we need to fix or mitigate them before we finalise our targets. That's what we cover in this step, Step 8: Fix Problems.

What happens in Step 8

We tackle the identified risks and issues by skipping back to the most appropriate previous step in the process to address each identified issue.

For example, if we discover an issue is best fixed by an extra KPI and target, we will head back to Step 2: Match KPIs, and use the KPI Tree to help us understand related KPIs that may help us counter the problem(s) we identified. We would then do a re-run of the subsequent steps for new KPI(s). It is generally much faster running through the steps for a second or third time as much of the hard work and discussion has already taken place — we just need to review the new elements we are introducing.

Sometimes it may take a few loops to iron out all of the potential issues. This may seem tedious, but it is much quicker and less painful than ironing these problems out <u>after</u> launch.

You will know you have completed the 'Fix Problems' step when no new issues are identified in Step 7: Black Hat Testing. At that point you can skip straight through this step and head on to Step 9: Record and Share Targets.

Case study example: Roughshod Repairs Call Centre

Roughshod

Repairs

Taking the issues Roger and the Roughshod team identified during black hat testing:

1. Insufficient allocated time for some types of calls.

The team were concerned that some calls require a longer handling time than 'allowed' to deal with the issue fully, compliantly, and in a customer-friendly way. Too little allocated handling time leads to at least two dysfunctional behaviours:

1a) Passing fixable calls to second-line support to stop the 'AHT clock' for the frontline agent - effectively making it someone else's problem (Output Misclassification DB-07 on the ROKET-DS™ Diagnostic)

1b) Rushing to close the call and/or cutting corners and alienating our customers in the process. Roger introduces the group to the ROKET-DS™ Diagnostic to explore what additional types of dysfunctional behaviour 'rushing to close the call' might drive. Led by the experienced call centre operations team members, the group conclude that agents would try and 'recover time' by:

- Skipping the legally required in-call disclaimers (Breaking the law DB-02)
- Cutting sections out of the mandatory call scripts (Rule breaking DB-03)
- Rushing call wrap-up to save time

The first two issues have potentially serious legal and regulatory implications, so are especially important to head off, before they become a real-world issue. All three problems create the risk of bad publicity and unhappy customers.

2. Increased customer call wait times (Time to answer)

The group is also concerned that a push on First Touch Resolution targets may blow the AHT targets and lead to call backlogs meaning longer wait times for customer calls to be answered, leading to angry customers and stressed agents.

The fix

Taking each of these issues and stepping back in the ROKET-DS™ process, let's look at the solution the team came up with for each of these issues:

1. Insufficient allowed time to handle some calls, handing fixable calls to second line support & rushing to close calls

There are two potential solutions to this.

A. Classify and target call lengths by call complexity. We can allow more time for more complex calls. The Roughshod Ops team have a good idea of which types of call take longer to resolve properly, so we can simply allow more time in the 'standard'. It makes the AHT calculation a bit more complicated, but it's fairer and it will encourage the right behaviours.

B. Attribute the whole call length to the initial handling agent, even when they hand it to second-line support. The operations team also know that a predictable percentage of calls will have to go to second line, and they can make a good estimate of what percentage this will be. Doing this removes the incentive to hand the call to second-line support as a way of 'stopping the clock'. Frontline agents will only hand a call to second line when it legitimately requires their extra skillset to resolve the call in the swiftest possible [overall] call time. It removes the driver to abuse the second-line support. Using this approach will mean that extra time will need to be factored into the AHT target to allow for the proportion of calls that will always need to be handed to second line, with the clock still running.

In the end, the Roughshod team decide to go with both options. The table below shows their revised targets for Average Handling Time, tiered based on complexity along with extra time factored in to allow for second-line support. There are three levels of performance too: solid, good, and legendary.

KPI	Level 1: Solid	Level 2: Good	Level 3: Legendary
First Touch Resolution	→ 65%	→ 75%	→ 80%
Average Handling Time Class 1	← 260 seconds	← 240 seconds	← 200 seconds
Average Handling Time Class 2	← 240 seconds	← 220 seconds	← 210 seconds
Average Handling Time Class 3	← 230 seconds	← 210 seconds	← 170 seconds

Making sure agents don't 'rush to close the call' and compromise customer interaction

The two solutions the group came up with for giving a fairer AHT should prevent some of the corner-cutting behaviours the group identified using the ROKET-DS™ Diagnostic, but we should still address these directly.

The team agree that 'rushed customer interaction' would not show up in our two proposed KPIs: AHT and FTR, and that they will probably need at least one more KPI.

They loop back to Step 2: Match KPIs and pull out the KPI Tree. Next, they ask themselves: "What KPIs do we have on our tree that could help us understand the quality of the call from a customer point of view?"

The post-call feedback score is a good starting point. If you've ever called a call centre, very often, you're asked to do a quick survey at the end of the call — that's what the post-call feedback score is, and this should give you a good idea of whether the customer is happy or not.

So, to mitigate the 'rushed customer interaction' risk, the team decide to target the end-of-call customer feedback score. They will use historic data to act as the baseline to set the 'solid', 'good', and 'legendary' target thresholds.

KPI	Level 1: Solid	Level 2: Good	Level 3: Legendary
First Touch Resolution	→ 65%	→ 75%	→ 80%
Average Handling Time Class 1	← 260 seconds	← 240 seconds	← 200 seconds
Average Handling Time Class 2	← 240 seconds	← 220 seconds	← 210 seconds
Average Handling Time Class 3	← 230 seconds	← 210 seconds	← 170 seconds
Customer Feedback Score	→ 80%	→ 83%	→ 87%

They also decide to include a target for the 'Call listening audit score' KPI. This score is awarded by one of Roughshod's training team after listening in on a live call. The trainer uses a structured marking scheme to determine the quality of the call. The target values the team agreed for this are shown in the final target table in the next section.

2. Longer call waits

If we target First Touch Resolution performance, we may find that the calls get longer with callers experiencing longer waits for their calls to be answered.

The Roughshod group had quite an animated discussion and debate on whether to target agents on a KPI called 'Grade of Service' (GoS).

> *'Grade of Service' is a KPI that shows the percentage of calls answered after a certain time — for example, a GoS of 80/20 is where at least 80% of calls are answered within 20 seconds.*

They even came up with the targets for this, but during the discussion, the group came to the conclusion that targeting agents on GoS is not fair.

Grade of Service is determined by two key factors: how much demand we have and our call handling capacity.

The agents answering the calls can influence the call duration (to some extent) but do not have agency over resource levels or demand levels, so the group decide not to add that to the agent scorecard. However, GoS will be part of the Operation Managers' targets, as they have full control over the resource/capacity part of the GoS calculation along with access to call volume forecasts.

Roughshod Repairs final KPI and target selections

These are the KPIs that they finalise at the end of Step 8:

- Average Handling Time, by agent
- First Touch Resolution rate, by agent
- Customer Feedback Score from the end of call survey, by agent

- Call Audit Listening Score, by agent

They decide not to measure Grade of Service because a large element of this KPI (centre capacity) is outside of the agent's control.

During 'Step 7: Black hat testing' and 'Step 8: Fixing problems' the group identified two extra KPIs and targets that are really going to help balance the overall performance, and are designed to stop agents from going to crazy extremes in an attempt to hit the Average Handling Time or First Touch Resolution targets.

Here is the final table of KPIs and targets that the Roughshod team agreed on:

KPI	Level 1: Solid	Level 2: Good	Level 3: Legendary
First Touch Resolution	→ 65%	→ 75%	→ 80%
Average Handling Time Class 1	← 260 seconds	← 240 seconds	← 200 seconds
Average Handling Time Class 2	← 240 seconds	← 220 seconds	← 210 seconds
Average Handling Time Class 3	← 230 seconds	← 210 seconds	← 170 seconds
Customer Feedback Score	→ 80%	→ 83%	→ 87%
Call Listening Audit Score	→ 70%	→ 75%	→ 80%

Our final step in the target design method is to share these newly minted targets with the wider team.

Nudge: Applying this to your targets

If you identified issues in black hat testing you should now develop rule tweaks and mitigations to curb those unintended behaviours and outcomes. Re-test the revised rules and capture those revisions in Box 8 of the ROKET-DS™ Target Design Canvas.

Part 2: How to design effective targets (or fix broken ones)

Step 9

Record &
go live

Step 9: Record and go live with targets

Once the targets have been designed and tested, the next step is to share those targets with the owners and to record them. The targets need to be more than accessible, they must be easily visible so the targets remain current and in the front of the team's minds. This means putting the targets on whiteboards, noticeboards, or live display screens. This also ensures there's no doubt or confusion about the actual target values. Displaying live performance versus target can be even more effective in motivating teams.

What happens in Step 9: Record and Share Targets

There are a few basic principles for recording and sharing our targets. Targets should be:

Shared with the right people

If we did 'Step 3: Identify and engage target stakeholders' correctly we should have no problem identifying the owners of the targets we have developed.

Clearly communicated and engaging

Without engagement from those responsible for achieving the targets, targets are useless. Target engagement is crucial and is built by:

- Identifying the correct stakeholders early in the target development process
- Doing a good job of identifying the right things to target and in coming up with realistic but ambitious target values
- Keeping all stakeholders up to date with target development through a sensible communications plan
- An honest, well-designed launch with plenty of opportunity for feedback and frank discussion

Highly visible and accessible

For targets to be effective, just 'existing' is not enough, they need to live in the mind of their owners. The best way to nurture this is to make sure the targets are highly visible, creating a 'cue' to develop an appropriate target 'habit'.

If we are displaying live performance, the most effective place to have your targets is visually, right next to the performance figure itself, or as a target bar on a chart.

We should check that:

- The target values are in a logical, convenient, and relevant place to compare with the relevant operational KPI
- There are no accessibility or visibility challenges for our target audience

Fully understood

It is important that those who own the performance targets understand their targets, the rules associated with those targets, and how the targets (and rules) were selected. We can do this via:

- A launch presentation or video
- A well-designed series of 'quick guides' explaining the target, how it was arrived at, and the 'rules'
- An FAQ document — covering 'frequently asked questions'

Fully documented

Like the rules of a board game, any ambiguity, contradiction, or loophole is likely to be quickly identified and exploited. We need to do our best to comprehensively record the 'rules' of our targets along with edge cases and complex special cases.

The ideal structure for recording your target design is the ROKET-DS™ Canvas (in your free download pack from **bettertargets.info** password **GAMED888**). The ROKET-DS™ Canvas covers all of the necessary fields, including the principles and logic behind the development of the canvas, which is perfect for supporting any subsequent review where the reviewers were not involved in the original target design and selection.

It is unusual to get everything right on the first go, so this documentation needs to be live and organic, but managed with discipline.

Options for recording your target documentation include:

- Notes or additional fields in your existing KPI definition management tool
- A specially created database, SharePoint site, or other type of collaborative document tool
- Well-designed 'quick guides' explaining the target, how it was arrived at, and the 'rules'. These can be in any easily shared document format, e.g. Microsoft Word, Adobe PDF etc. Just be mindful of access and content protection.
- An FAQ document — covering 'frequently asked questions'
- A wiki, with all the relevant information and a knowledge base covering the rules and special cases
- Contextual help in your reporting or dashboard tool

Secure and authentic, with managed updates and versioning

When we make changes and updates to our targets, we need to version control lists. Anyone who has sat an exam would probably love to be able to change the grade boundaries. If our targets have got big rewards or big downsides, then we need to make sure that they don't creep up or creep down through anonymous edits and changes, so we need a single version of the truth and we need access control. We must make sure that everyone who needs to see the targets can see them, but the ability to control them or edit them is restricted and protected.

We must make sure that the versions of targets in use are correct and original, and have not been altered or adjusted in an unauthorised way. Options include, but aren't limited to:

- Documents in a shared folder with appropriate read-write user access permissions
- A SharePoint (or similar) site with appropriate user read-write access rights
- An intranet page with clearly defined ownership and update permissions
- A locked glass display board (very 1970s, simple but effective)

We should also make sure that we have a maintained backup of any system that we use to store our targets, given the substantial effort that goes into creating targets, fully documenting them, and creating a maintained knowledge base.

- Is the recording location secure?
- Do we have a backup system in place?
- Do we have an archive process for superseded targets?
- Is the recording location known by a number of people — if a key person leaves will anyone else know where they are stored?

Implementing incentives too?

If you are implementing incentives to sit alongside targets, you may choose to do your implementation and communications planning for targets and incentives together, in which case you can do everything in Step 14.

Sharing your targets as OKRs

OKRs are a popular way of expressing objectives and targets. John Doerr, author of bestseller Measure What Matters, describes them as

> ...a collaborative goal-setting tool used by teams and individuals to set challenging, ambitious goals with measurable results. OKRs are how you track progress, create alignment, and encourage engagement around measurable goals.

What does an OKR look like?

Here's an example. If I wanted to reduce my risk of heart disease, my OKR might look like this:

Objective: Improve my cardiac risk profile

Key result 1: Hit a body mass index of 22 by losing 10kg

Key result 2: Reduce my blood pressure to an average of 120/80 or lower

Key result 3: Reduce my total cholesterol to 5 or lower

You will notice some familiar elements here:

Identifying a problem or outcome: Step 1 of the ROKET-DS™ approach

Matching KPIs to the outcome: An OKR is a high-level objective paired with lower-level results which will deliver that objective. In Step 2 of the ROKET-DS™ method we use a KPI Tree to create a rich visual representation of the relationship between my top-level outcome, the drivers of that outcome, and the KPIs that indicate those drivers are heading in the right direction.

Setting ambitious targets: Once the objectives and drivers have been identified, the final part of OKR design is to set ambitious targets. We took plenty of care in Steps 4–8 to identify targets that were sensible but challenging.

Having worked your way through Steps 1–8 of the ROKET-DS™ method you will have everything you need to package your targets as OKRs. Using the OKR format, or not, comes down entirely to personal and organisational preference. If you do go down the OKR route, don't forget to make sure you cover all the other practical sharing and management points covered in the 'Implementation Checklist'.

Case study example: Roughshod Repairs Call Centre

Roughshod

Repairs

Step 9 — record and share targets — is quite straightforward for Roughshod. Following the steps in the key points from the previous section:

Shared with the right people

At the start of the process, Ruby and the team built a stakeholder list. The developed targets are directly relevant to all the centre agents and their supervisors. The operations managers are also important stakeholders when it comes to messaging and enforcement.

Clearly communicated and engaging

Ruby's team put together a simple communications plan, in which they have the following:

- An initial announcement that targets are under development
- Regular updates and presentations from the team through the weekly centre update town hall, particularly focusing on the business goals the targets will be supporting
- Targets' launch by the centre manager, again emphasising the importance of the targets in supporting the security and growth of Roughshod Repairs
- Cascade of detailed targets to each team through the team communications cascade

Highly visible and accessible

The targets are clearly visible on each agent's computer screen, alongside their current shift performance and monthly average. There is a help link immediately next to each target which takes the agent to a wiki that has been set up by the team, with target explanations and FAQs.

Fully understood

The target development team have created a large foam-board explainer board. They have taken all of the management team through it, to team leader level, drilled the team leaders on delivering the 'explainer' and recorded an explanation video that is now on the intranet.

Each team leader is tasked with explaining their target to the team, dealing with any questions and referring any tough questions to the target development team.

Fully documented

A SharePoint sheet has been set up with all the fields from the ROKET-DS™ Target Canvas. Each field from the Canvas is populated with a full explanation and maintained.

Secure and authentic, with managed updates and versioning

The current live targets are shared on a purpose-built wiki, powered by Microsoft SharePoint.

Whenever a new version of a target is released, version control information is recorded privately showing:

- Modification owner
- Who requested the modification
- When the modification came into effect
- Why the modification was made and what the intended effect was

In Part 3, we will go into a lot more detail about how people will be <u>rewarded</u> for hitting their respective targets, but at this stage, don't worry about it.

Nudge: Applying this to your targets

Time to record and share targets. How will targets be stored and shared? How will you manage changes and updates? Now is also the time to think about how the rollout will be <u>communicated</u>. Use the GAMED Design and Implementation Checklists to help you do this and record the headlines in Box 9 of the ROKET-DS™ Target Design Canvas.

How often should you set and review targets?

A common challenge is deciding <u>how often</u> to review targets. Targets are designed to help us **control** or **improve** something we care about.

Let's look at two examples.

Example 1. Heart rate versus target during major surgery

- It's very important
- It can change in seconds
- We need to know if it's outside of the target range immediately as we have only a few minutes to fix things if the heart stops

For all of these reasons patient heart rate needs to be measured and compared with the target in <u>real-time</u> for major surgery.

Example 2. Patient weight during major surgery

- Patient weight affects complexity and success of many types of surgery. It is important
- Patient weight changes over weeks, months or years
- It takes weeks or months to reduce excess weight

A single weight measurement before surgery would be enough to compare patient weight with surgical guidelines. So, despite being **important**, patient weight would not need to be measured at all during surgery.

The three target frequency questions

We used three simple questions to make that decision on target review frequency:

1. How important is the measure?
2. How fast can it go wrong?
3. How much notice do we need to fix it, to keep it in control?

Try and resist the urge to make all your target review schedules fit with your existing meeting schedules, typically daily, weekly, or monthly. While doing this will make things simpler to schedule, it will not always deliver the best outcomes.

Optional Section: Habits, compulsion and targets

We are what we repeatedly do. Excellence, then, is not an act, but a habit.

Often attributed to Aristotle, but by William Durant, paraphrasing Aristotle in The Story of Philosophy, 1926

Why is it I check my email inbox several times a day but shy away from weighing myself?

What makes social media so irresistible, yet expensive home-gym equipment often sits around, barely used?

The answer to these questions lies in the formation of <u>habits</u> and the way our brains seek rewards. The addictiveness of social media is not an accident, it's the prized outcome of very careful design.

What have habits got to do with targets? A target that is never reviewed or acted upon might as well not exist. Worse than that, an unreviewed KPI and target is a kind of 'tax' on the organisation, a costly set of information that was never looked at or acted upon.

Forming a 'review habit', particularly for short-term KPIs and targets, is an essential behavioural requirement to enable KPIs to have a positive impact on your business performance.

The challenge

To be effective, some targets and KPIs need regular review and action. Often these are focused on operational measures, like queue length, wait times or stock levels.

If we want to steer team actions and behaviours using short-term KPIs and targets, we need to make looking at those figures as hard to resist as glancing at your phone for new emails, checking your smart watch activity score for the day or checking your social media feed.

Let's just be clear on what we mean by a 'habit'. The definition I use is:

Behaviours done with little or no conscious thought

From 'Hooked' by Nir Eyal

Most of the published work in the field of creating habit-forming products looks at software products, so we need a little lateral thinking to understand how those insights apply to KPIs and performance reports. The good news is that one of the most commonly used methodologies is fairly easily adapted to our needs.

Three steps to strengthen your KPI habits

Behavioural research has shown that there are several ways you can nurture or destroy habit formation. Anyone who has raised children may well already have figured out the critical steps through trial and error.

Step 1: Be specific about the type of behaviour you want

Be as clear as possible and don't make people think too hard.

Break down your strategic objectives into 'bite-sized chunks' - clear and specific behaviours and activities that will help you achieve your objective.

How to apply this...

There's a huge difference between saying...

I'd like the team to do a regular performance review

and...

I would like <u>you</u> (the team leader) to run a standing-up review twice a shift, on the hour, following this agenda. It must last no more than 5 mins and cover these performance measures and targets.

Which instruction is most likely to lead to a regular routine and ultimately the formation of a habit?

Step 2: Make it easy to do the right thing

The easier you make it, the more likely it is to happen.

How can you remove obstacles and make the right behaviour easy to do?

Encouraging the desired behaviour has a few angles:

- **Time**. The longer something takes the less likely people are to do it.
- **Money**. If there is some direct cost involved in the behaviour (for example, having to make a call using their own phone) or indirect cost (missing out on overtime) it will act as a strong disincentive to take action and ultimately not form a habit. Will they gain financially from doing it, for example hitting a team performance target?
- **Physical effort**. If the action you intend to make into a habit involves having to walk up some stairs, get out of a chair, or go out in the cold — i.e. physical effort or discomfort — it will <u>discourage</u> habit formation.

- **Brain effort**. Having to think too hard puts people off taking action. This brain-effort deterrent becomes even stronger if people are tired and/or busy.

How might this translate into practice for performance measurement and management?

For reviewing target values:

- Make the target and KPI visible without any effort on the user's part (minimise physical effort).
- Present the KPI and the target right next to each other (minimise brain effort).
- Use chart techniques, like target bars, to give a visual representation of the gap between the KPI and the target (minimise brain effort).

Step 3: Make sure the behaviour is triggered

What will activate the desired behaviour? All behaviours require a trigger, sometimes the trigger is internal, sometimes external.

What exactly are triggers?

Triggers are the nudge to take action. It may be as simple as a reminder popping up on a screen, an email landing in your inbox, or a team leader prompting the team to do something. Our lives are filled with triggers, but we often barely notice them. For many, their day starts with an external trigger (alarm clock goes off) and is followed by a firework display of internal triggers that get us washed, dressed, and packed for the day ahead. The best triggers are ones that are sparked by your own memory or by some minor but reliable environmental factor.

Triggers are the vital final step in our habit-forming method, our cue to take action. Triggers fall into two camps:

- External triggers tell us what to do next by placing a prompt or information in the user's environment. Alarm clocks, to-do lists, timed texts, smart watch alerts, calendar alerts, or Post-its on your PC monitor all fall into this category.

- Internal triggers prompt the user on what to do next through associations stored in their memory. Going into the bathroom first thing in the morning will trigger you to remember to clean your teeth. Leaving the house will remind you to check you have your keys, phone, and wallet. We have thousands of internal triggers every day but, because of their nature, they are almost imperceptible to us.

Quite often we use a mixture of internal and external triggers.

I have to remember to look at my to-do task manager on my phone but, once I remember to do this, there is a list of 'External triggers' to get me to act on my tasks.

What does this mean in practice for performance measurement and management?

There are a selection of external triggers we can use:

- Calendar reminders
- Meetings
- Agenda items (though there often needs to be a pre-meeting trigger, otherwise this just catches out the unwary)
- Performance boards
- Alarms

Formal performance reviews are fine, and a good start, but targets and KPIs become much more useful and powerful when they become a seamless part of our view on the world.

Our ultimate goal must be to create internal triggers. These are more powerful and do not require sustained effort or vigilance once they are established — just some occasional nurturing and care to make sure we don't accidentally break them.

Visual prompts can be a very good way of sparking internal triggers. A well-placed performance board can really grease the wheels when it comes to forming internal KPI review triggers.

How to tell when 'triggers' have become internal

Our end goal is for everyone in the team to be actively 'pulling' performance information. When a team member walks in, do they request and show a genuine interest in the performance figures? Do the shop floor team show a keen interest in how the day's figures are progressing, how they are doing compared with other teams, whether they are close to breaking a record? When performance figures are referred to in everyday work conversation you know that you are well on your way to building 'the KPI and target habit'.

Recap: ROKET-DS™ target design method

That brings us to the end of the ten-step target design method. For many of you, this will be a major milestone on the way to designing your incentives. For others, setting targets may have been your sole goal.

Let's just review and recap the purpose and highlights of each step in the method so far...

Step 0	Step 1	Step 2	Step 3	Step 4
Identify existing issues	Plan outcome	Match KPIs	Identify & engage target owners	Check owner agency

Step 5	Step 6	Step 7	Step 8	Step 9
Draft target values & rules	White hat test targets	Black hat test targets	Fix problems & re-test	Record & go live

Step 0: Identify existing issues

If you have existing targets with problems you start at Step 0. In this step we identify and document those problems. You can also use the ROKET-DS™ Diagnostic to help flush out any other related issues.

Step 1: Plan outcome

When you don't have existing targets and incentives, then you start at Step 1. In this step we identify the high-level outcomes that we're looking for. These are six high-level outcomes — e.g., Growth, Manage Risk and so — labelled the 'Big 6' to help us rapidly identify common strategic outcomes. Some mission-based organisations will need an extra one or two custom objectives that are specific to their 'mission'.

Step 2: Match KPIs

In Step 2, we identify the family of KPIs that we need to target to achieve our strategic outcome. You can either:

1. Agree a handful of best KPIs to indicate your strategic outcome through <u>discussion</u> (small organisations or simple scenarios).

2. Use a KPI Tree to identify the relevant and related KPIs that will show you if you're on track for achieving the high-level goal from Step 1. KPI Trees are a rich and powerful way of understanding the links between performance and outcome, but they do take time and effort. KPI Trees are most useful for larger organisations or complex situations. To find out more about KPI Trees head to madetomeasurekpis.com/kpi-tree-intro.

Step 3: Identify and engage target owners

In this step we identify everyone who can influence the KPIs we identified in the previous step, Match KPIs, and decide how and when we will communicate and engage with them.

Step 4: Check owner agency

Review our KPIs and planned outcomes to see if the target owners have the necessary <u>agency</u>. Agency is the ability to deliver the target result and includes skills, time, authority, and resources (STAR). If your target owners don't have agency, you need to fix it. Targeting and incentivising people who don't have full agency is dangerous as it often leads to burnout, rule breaking, and even illegal behaviour.

Step 5: Set draft target values

Next you draft your initial values and rules for your targets. We need to decide whether we're going to use 'all or nothing' targets or perhaps tiered targets where we have different levels. Use historic data wherever possible when you're setting your draft targets; it gives a starting point for assessing what is <u>achievable</u>.

Step 6: White hat testing

In Step 6, you walk through what should happen if the target owners follow the process in the <u>expected way</u>, with no attempt to game or test the target rule set.

Step 7: Black hat testing

In 'Step 7: Black hat testing' you get a little evil and ask, "In the real world, if we had to achieve these targets by <u>any means necessary</u>, how would we do that?" Use reverse brainstorming and the ROKET-DS™ Diagnostic to help flush out potential problems and solutions.

Step 8: Fix problems and re-test

Once you've identified potential problems using black hat testing, you need to skip back either to Step 2 (Match KPIs) or to Step 5 (Set draft target values), depending on whether you need additional KPIs or to rework KPI targets. Then, rework the subsequent steps in the process until you get back to black hat testing. If you clear black hat testing with no issues, you are ready to head to our next step — Step 9: Record and Share Targets.

Step 9: Record and share targets

Once you've tested and tweaked your KPIs, you've got your final target values and they get through black hat testing unscathed, it's time to record them in an accessible place, to share them, and to manage any post-launch updates and adjustments in a secure and open way.

There's a lot to remember, so don't forget that you have access to the ROKET-DS™ Target Design canvas in the free download pack that accompanies this book. You will find a similar canvas for incentive design as well. These canvases come as a pair, but at the moment, we've only covered the 'target design' part of the method.

When you come to build your own targets, I'd recommend printing out both design canvases (A3/Tabloid works well, A2 is even better) and then put them on the wall. The team can write on it, add stickies, and use it as a focal point for workshops. The canvas will also guide you through the questions you need to ask in order to get good quality, effective, robust targets.

In your download folder, you will find a version of this canvas that has already been completed for Roughshod Repair. You will see the case study that we have just worked through, laid out in the ROKET-DS™ canvas format, which can used be a handy reference tool and memory jogger.

Congratulations. That wraps up the target design section. Stay with us though, as our next section is all about the weird, wonderful, and interesting world of incentive design. Incentives are the lightning bolt that will bring your new target creation to life.

Part 3: How to design effective incentives (or fix broken ones)

In this section we will explore...

- How we expect incentives to work and the ways in which they often go wrong
- The motivational foundations that incentives theory is built on, which will help explain some of the unexpected behaviour often seen
- The rules of incentive design, developed from academic research in the field

All of this motivational goodness is then rolled into a five-step process that is designed to follow straight on from where the target design process in Part 2 left off.

Key incentive concepts...

Refresher: What is an incentive?

If the KPI provides the objective <u>truth</u>, and the target provides the <u>context</u> then an incentive is intended to provide the <u>behavioural motivation</u>. An incentive can be either positive (I buy myself a new smart watch if I hit 80kg), negative/punitive (I will put a padlock on the fridge if I hit 85 kg) or some combination of the two.

The motivation model we all use without thinking

There is a seductively simple model that most of us use for targets, incentives, and behaviour. The logic goes like this...

If we want someone to do something, we set them a target and offer a reward for achieving that target or punish them for not achieving it.

Put a little more reductively...

[Target] + [Reward for hitting target] and/or [Penalty for missing target] drives [Desired behaviour] which delivers [Desired outcome]

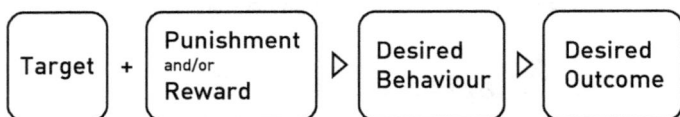

Target + Punishment and/or Reward ▷ Desired Behaviour ▷ Desired Outcome

Everybody from parents of young children through to reforming governments invest a huge amount of time, effort, and energy based on the assumed truth of this model.

- If the target is important, we offer a valuable reward, often money.
- If we <u>really</u> want them to achieve the target, we offer them a <u>bigger</u> reward.
- If we want people to over-perform, we offer additional financial incentives.

Whether it's banks offering bonuses to their staff or governments incentivising couples to have children, this approach seems to be hard-wired into most business models and even our personal lives.

The risk of using high-value incentives

There are two major risks that come from using classic incentives where the reward has high real-world monetary value or extreme reward and recognition (think 'winning the Olympics', officially the only reward is a medal, but in reality the rewards are much more tangible and often financial) .

Classic reward incentives often <u>do not work</u> and frequently have the opposite effect from the intended one.

Highly desirable rewards can drive cheating, use of loopholes, and even law-breaking. Policing high-value incentives can introduce an extra level of stress, complexity, and cost.

Why do rewards often fail, backfire and become difficult to run? That's what we will explore in this chapter.

The two types of motivation

Intrinsic and extrinsic motivation: their critical differences

Our classic model assumes a particular <u>type</u> of motivation, called 'extrinsic' motivation. This type of motivation is the sort that comes from external reward or punishment. The logic is that if you offer a big enough reward, it drives someone to do something that you want them to do.

There is another type of motivation, the sort that drives amateurs to...

- Complete a tough non-competitive run
- Climb a mountain
- Learn an instrument

These are complex, demanding tasks where the rewards are non-financial and usually come from <u>within</u> the individual. These people are prepared to put hours of training and effort into something where the reward is entirely <u>internal</u>.

This type of internal motivation is called **intrinsic motivation**. It's the sort of motivation that comes from personal challenge and the satisfaction that arises from meeting that challenge.

Why external reward (or punishment) is not always a good idea

There have been many psychological experiments on the relationship between intrinsic and extrinsic motivation and their results uncover an interesting, and surprising, risk.

In the 1973 Stanford experiment by Lepper, Greene and Nisbett, researchers decided to see what impact external reward had on a 'fun' activity for a group of preschoolers.[18]

They came up with an optional activity that they had previously shown kids would be interested in: using felt-tip pens and a big pile of paper to draw pictures.

The experiment had three groups.

- The first group, the 'Expected award' group, were told at the start that they would be given a 'Good player award' for their drawings, once the six minute session was complete.
- The second group, the 'Unexpected award' group, were awarded a 'Good player award' after drawing a picture, and were given no advance warning of a reward.
- The third group, the 'No award' group, were simply allowed to draw with no award promised or given.

During the experiment, children who were in the 'Expected award group' scored <u>worse</u> during the test (on 'blind quality' scoring) and after the assessment showed a <u>reduced interest</u> in the activity that they previously enjoyed, compared with the other two groups.

The introduction of the promise of external reward before the activity worsened performance in the short term and reduced interest in the activity in the longer term. The researchers gave this effect the name 'Overjustification'.

In another study of the effects of rewards on the motivation of adults, by Edward Deci[19] in 1971, students were asked to do a puzzle (with the competing lure of magazines on the table next to them). The experimental group worked for three sessions and were paid on a 'per solution' basis in the second session. Their motivation was measured based on their engagement with the puzzle during 'downtime' when they didn't realise they were part of the experiment.

The results showed that when reward money was involved, intrinsic motivation <u>declined</u>. When 'verbal reinforcement and positive feedback' was used, motivation <u>increased</u>.

This study suggests that the <u>type</u> of reward also has an impact on intrinsic motivation.

The message here is that any type of reward has the potential to undermine a person's inbuilt (intrinsic) interest in an activity and monetary rewards can have a particularly harmful impact.

The <u>cost</u> of incentives

A tale of two events

Running is a popular sport. It has a low barrier to entry and is probably the oldest competitive athletic activity. It's also a useful lab to compare two very different approaches to incentives.

Olympic running

Anyone not living in a cave for the past hundred years will be aware that running is a major part of the Olympics. The 100m sprint and marathon are centrepieces of the event. Victory in the Olympics can bring immense fame and fortune. The sprinting legend Usain Bolt is estimated to have a net worth of over $90 million.[20]

In the 2018 Winter Olympics timekeeping was handled by 300 timekeepers, supported by 350 trained volunteers and 230 tonnes of equipment.[21] Performance-enhancing substance testing was run by the World Anti-Doping Agency (WADA), which had an annual budget of $32 million (2018) and employed 117 full-time staff. [22]

Parkrun

At the other end of the spectrum is a UK grassroots running movement called parkrun. Across 700+ UK locations, thousands of runners head to their local parks each weekend to run (or walk) timed 5k races. There's no fee and the only reward is a free t-shirt after 50, 100, 250 and 500 races and a record of your race time on the parkrun website. It is run by thousands of <u>unpaid</u> volunteers.

Timekeeping is handled using (optional) personal bar codes to log your time with a scanner-wielding volunteer at the end of your race. The only performance-enhancing substances found on parkrun are usually coffee and homemade cake. Needless to say, there's no testing programme for this.

And the difference is...

The core activity of both movements is the same: running. The difference lies in the types (and magnitude) of incentives and rewards on offer. Although the Olympics was designed originally for 'amateurs', it is no secret that winning a high profile event brings international fame and riches (afterwards), extrinsic rewards. These extreme rewards have driven behaviours that have led to the need for multi-million dollar timekeeping and anti-doping measures for elite sports around the world. For parkrun, there are no prizes beyond a token free t-shirt for 50+ runs and the satisfaction that comes from running a good time. There is no fame or fortune attached to an outstanding parkrun. Activities that are based on intrinsic motivation, like parkrun, are far cheaper and simpler to police than activities with substantial material rewards, such as a flagship Olympic event.

Incentives and the baggage they bring

Incentives can stimulate dramatic responses. Whether it's the prospect of earning lots of cash, fame, or the threat of dire consequences, some people will take much more extreme measures when there is a strong incentive or punishment in place.

Put simply, the bigger the reward or penalty the greater the likelihood of...

- Loopholes being identified
- Rule-breaking
- Law-breaking (in extreme circumstances)

Of course, it's possible to tighten the rules, police those rules more carefully and create deterrents to offset the temptation to cheat, but this all takes time, effort, and money. As any fan of motor racing will also know, it's rarely a static situation. Racing teams constantly test the limits of the rules in new and creative ways, leading to a kind of 'arms race' when it comes to creating and flexing maker's rules.

Any major performance-based incentive will bring with it a significant cost of policing and enforcement, in addition to the costs of the incentive itself.

Serious extrinsic incentives bring risk

Larger extrinsic incentives do not just bring greater enforcement cost and complexity, they bring additional risk. No policing system is perfect, so we must ask:

"What risky behaviours and outcomes may be incentivised by this? And, what are the reputational, legal, and moral implications of those risks?"

As we saw in our earlier case studies, these risks can sometimes be measured in terms of employee years in prison, avoidable deaths, or losses of tens of billions of dollars.

The most important incentive design decision

This is the most important decision you will make when you are setting up your targets.

'Will you offer a reward with significant monetary value or prestige for achieving the set targets?'

This single decision will have a <u>profound</u> effect on how your targets and incentives function, whether they deliver the intended results, and repay the effort required to manage them.

In this section we will introduce a five-step method that will help you develop effective incentives for <u>any</u> situation. Most of the steps will feel very familiar if you have worked your way through the Target Design method earlier in this book. What will be new is the first step in the incentive design process: 'Draft incentives, values and rules'. This step is the heart of the ROKET-DS™ Incentive Design method and is made of up of eight principles to help you design effective incentives.

The eight principles of incentive design

There's been a substantial amount of academic work on incentives, in particular sales incentives. Although this research is very useful, it can be a little bit dry and difficult to digest.

To make things simpler and more readable we have created a fictional case study based on a sales team at Shizzle Systems, a completely fictional mid-sized US software vendor that specialises in manufacturing planning software.

Shizzle Systems sales incentives case study

Siddharth, or Sid as everyone knows him, is the hero of our story. He's the Sales Director of Shizzle Systems. Sid has a team of 20 sales executives and some very aggressive profit targets from his board. He has been running the sales team for four years with mixed results. Here is his journey.

In the beginning...

Four years ago, when Sid took over the team it was barely a sales team. There were half a dozen team members, mostly 'user-friendly' sales support staff who had fallen into the role. In a nod towards managing the sales process, his predecessor had introduced 'token' sales rewards, prizes like a crate of beer, tickets to a football match, or a meal for two. These prizes had become a running joke in the office, with a wheelbarrow appearing in the office one morning with the label 'bonus shifter' emblazoned on it.

Over the next two years, Sid grew the team to twenty sales execs and overhauled the sales incentive scheme. He named this new programme 'Shizzle Stars Sales Rewards'.

First attempt: Shizzle Stars Sales Rewards

After some thought and looking at incentive schemes in similar organisations, Sid decided to offer sales prizes, a proper commission scheme, a bonus, and to trim the number of sales execs on the team.

The sales prizes: Sid set up three prizes for best sales performance. The centrepiece of Shizzle Stars Sales Rewards was a week-long five-star resort vacation in Hawaii for the star sales executive and their partner. Second place was five nights in a four-star hotel in a local national park for two people, and third place was a voucher for two nights in a national hotel chain for two.

Next, he introduced a sales commission that kicked in at 100% of target and topped out at 125% of target. The target for the year was based on 125% of the team's average performance last year, so an individual would need to hit that figure before they started earning commission.

Sid also created an annual bonus scheme, partly based on sales performance but also including key account development and demonstration of company values.

As part of his 'new broom' approach, Sid fired three of his weakest players. He felt Shizzle was over-resourced in sales and cutting these roles enabled him to fund the new incentives scheme at zero net cost. He also felt that the new prize offers, along with firing the weakest players, would 'encourage' the survivors to make up the loss.

Over the following 12 months, it all went horribly wrong.

This Shizzle Explodes...

Initially, there was excitement. Shizzle Stars was launched over a team meal, with some fine words delivered by the CEO, endorsing the approach. After a few short months things deteriorated and after the first annual 'Shizzle Star Prize Awards' the team started bailing out, in droves. Sales performance was flat, morale was low, and the finance department were complaining to Sid on a regular basis about the money that was being 'wasted' on commission and frivolous prizes. They were pushing aggressively to reduce the commission rate and downsize the prizes.

1. Two of the three 'Superstars' in the team left, moaning about capped commission.

2. The midrange performers, a group dubbed the 'Foot Soldiers' by Sid, complained that it was always the same 'teachers' pets' that won the prizes. Most of them hit their targets but didn't seem bothered about trying to 'up their game'.

3. The weakest performers, a group Sid called the 'Laggards', all fell short of their sales targets and moaned constantly about not seeing any commission or having any chance of winning prizes.

4. The people who won the second and third prizes privately grumbled about getting 'crappy consolation prizes'.

Sid was bewildered. How could such a carefully designed approach deliver such an unhappy team and zero performance improvement?

Why it went wrong

Sid decided to dig into the research on sales targets and incentives to try and figure out why Shizzle Stars had gone so horribly wrong. As he reviewed the research, he had a creeping feeling of horror as he realised why things had turned out so badly...

Project Shangri-La: Bringing the fizzle back to Shizzle

Principle 1: Portfolio management — don't just focus on one group

Within any sales team there will always be Superstars, Foot Soldiers, and Laggards. Although it's tempting to focus on the Superstars, the majority of selling is often done by the large body of Foot Soldiers. Neglecting the Foot Soldiers and Laggards is a mistake.

The Shizzle Stars' prize focus was entirely on the top performers, leaving the Foot Soldiers and Laggards without prizes or the hope of winning a prize. The Laggards were not just out of the running for prizes, they also stood little chance of earning significant commission.

To tackle this, Sid decides to treat the sales team as a portfolio of investments, treating each group as distinct entities and handling them in a customised way.

Principle 2: Tiered targets and prizes — don't just motivate your top performers

A tiered scheme might look like this:

First tier — set at a level that most of the sales team achieved over the last two years

Second tier — tougher but still achieved by about 20% of the team

Third tier — only for the elite superstar sales team members

The idea is to have 'something for everyone'. Research shows that the elite salespeople are motivated to push themselves even harder by the exclusive and impressive Tier 3 incentive. The Foot soldiers aim for Tier 2 and the Laggards will be motivated by the really quite achievable Tier 1 reward and are satisfied when they hit it.

Problem: In the Shizzle Stars programme the sales targets were all stretch targets based on the team average, so hitting 100% felt like it was out of reach for most of the team, so they ceased to be a motivator — especially for the weakest performers.

Solution: Introduce a three-tier approach, with aspirational prizes for the Superstars, Foot Soldiers and the Laggards.

Principle 3: Multiple prizes — differentiate, don't downgrade

Offering prizes to each ability level within the team comes with a few risks. The prize for the top performance needs to be more prestigious and covetable than for the prize for Foot Soldiers and Laggards but needs to be chosen in a way that does not make the winners of the Tier 1 and 2 prizes feel that they are just inferior versions of the Tier 3 prize.

The way to do this is to offer <u>distinct</u> types of prizes.

Problem: From the sales team's perspective, it was very obvious to the second and third place winners that they had won the consolation prize, a prize that was clearly a downgraded version of the first prize.

As a reminder, here are the original Shizzle Stars Sales Reward prizes:

A. A week-long five-star resort vacation in Hawaii for the star sales executive and their partner

B. A five night stay in a four-star hotel in a local national park for two

C. A voucher for two nights in a national hotel chain for two

This approach devalued the impact of those prizes to the runners-up.

Solution: To tackle this, Sid changed the prizes:

- The Tier 3 (top) prize remained a week-long five-star resort vacation in Hawaii for two.
- The Tier 2 prize was changed to a Super-Car Track Day, rather than a downgraded vacation. The winner of the Tier 2 prize can then rationalise their prize by saying that they prefer the excitement of a driving experience to the hassle and effort of an overseas holiday.
- Using the same thought-process, the Tier 1 prize became a three-course meal for two — the third-place winner can justify the attractiveness of the prize by saying to themselves that it will give them a chance to spend time with their partner, rather than running off to have fun on their own with the driving prize.

Whilst the Tier 3 prize is clearly the most impressive in terms of cost, it's perfectly possible for the winners of the Tier 2 and 1 prizes to rationalise that, in fact, they prefer their prize, increasing the chance that all parties can be happy with their reward.

Principle 4: Setting the pace — getting more from the poorest performers

The longer the gap between what we do and the reward, the weaker the impact of that reward becomes. The time period between bonuses can have a major impact on motivation.

Research by Thomas Steenburgh[23] found that switching from a quarterly bonus to an annual bonus had the most significant negative impact on your bottom performers. The Laggards performance dropped by about 10%, the Foot Soldiers performance drop-off was 4% and for the Superstars it was just 2%.

So, all groups benefit from having more frequent incentive payments, but it particularly encourages the poorest performers in any team.

Problem: In Shizzle Stars, Sid had set the commission scheme to quarterly payments and the bonus scheme to annual review, with payment 3 months after review.

Solution: After reading about Steenburgh's work, Sid switched to monthly commission payments and quarterly bonus reviews and payments (as the process is quite manual and monthly reviews would be too time consuming for everyone).

Principle 5: Feeling the heat — social pressure keeps 'em keen

An oversupply of high quality talent tends to have a motivating effect on the existing workforce. This doesn't just apply to sales. In Formula One engineering teams, where there is an almost limitless pool of talented motivated engineers craving jobs in elite motorsports, we see this displayed as an established culture of very long work hours for relatively modest pay.

The same seems to apply in sales. Analysis shows that salespeople in districts where there were 'spare players' performed about 5% better than those without available surplus resource. This effect has the biggest impact on the lowest performers, the laggards. So, although it may look like we're carrying expensive extra resources it may actually make economic sense to have a few spare bodies on the team, as long as they are decent performers.

Problem: Sid decided to trim the sales team as a means of funding the Shizzle Stars programme. Looking back, he is convinced that this removed some psychological pressure from his remaining weak performers.

Solution: Based on this research, Sid decides that he will make sure he replaces one of the leavers with one, perhaps two, strong players from outside of Shizzle Systems creating some psychological pressure on the current team members.

Principle 6: Making the most of your Superstars — don't cap commission

There seems to be some kind of innate resistance to paying other human beings large amounts of money, even when it makes perfect sense to do so. This particularly applies to sales commission and seems to occur for two reasons:

1. The figures involved can be large for a Superstar salesperson
2. There is often strong resistance to big commission payments from those who assess <u>cost</u> — typically the finance department

Your star performers are the people most likely to hit commission caps, and yet this doesn't make rational sense. As long as paying a bonus does not incur a loss on each sale, more sales should be a good thing for both parties.

Research by Sanjog Misra and Harikesh Nair shows that the difference between capped and uncapped sales commission makes a 9% difference to total revenue.

Problem: A few years ago, the star sales executive turned up in new Porsche 911 Turbo, shortly afterwards the Shizzle Systems Finance department insisted on a commission cap to 'keep costs under control'. That cap has persisted.

Solution: Sid raises the idea of removing the sales commission cap, making sure commission is paid on profitability not contract value with his CEO, using the research evidence to support his case. He also suggested that the commission fees be excluded from the Finance department's cost management targets. His CEO agrees to give it a trial.

So, the headline is: "Don't cap sales commission if you want to maximise revenue". In fact...

Principle 7: Reward overachievement <u>more</u>, not less

Offering an higher rate of commission, for sales above a threshold (for example the sales target) can drive sales overachievement. Another study by Thomas Steenburgh shows that, for an office supply company, paying an enhanced commission for sales <u>above</u> quota contributed an additional 17% to the Superstar sales figures.

Problem: Even with the removal of the commission cap, Sid wants to get the most he can out of his Superstars.

Solution: Sid decides to offer an extra 20% on the commission rate when a sales exec goes 25% above profit target, rising to 30% when over 50% of target and maxing out at 40% uplift for profit over 200% of target.

Principle 8: Spread the love — multiple winners, everyone wins

Work by Noah Lim has shown that having multiple prizes will boost performance more than one, epic, 'winner takes all' prize. One conclusion of their study was that there should be at least as many prizes as there are Superstars — increasing the likelihood that a Foot Soldier or Laggard will win a prize — so keeping the pressure on the Superstars to perform.

Problem: Shizzle offered three prizes, but Shizzle has four Superstar players, so more Superstars than prizes. This meant that it was highly predictable who would win the prizes. As the prizes were announced the solid Foot Soldiers and Laggards rolled their eyes, shot some meaningful looks to each other, and got back to checking their iPhones. This was not turning into the competitive motivator Sid intended it to be.

Solution: Reading about Lim's research, Sid realises that this leaves the Foot Soldiers with little realistic chance of winning a prize. Being careful to differentiate the prizes in terms of type, as well as value, Sid expands the prize scheme to include <u>five</u> prizes, up from the three he had originally planned.

The launch

This time round, Sid goes for a much more low-key launch, carefully walking each member of the team through the new programme, one on one, dealing with questions and concerns as openly and honestly as he can.

Despite his cautious launch, he's much more confident that his approach will yield decent results this time round. After his last one-to-one briefing session, he kicks back in his chair and starts to daydream about his future Lamborghini.

Recap: The Motive8 Principles

Principle 1: Portfolio management — don't just focus on one group

Within any sales team there will always be Superstars, Foot Soldiers, and Laggards.

Treat the sales team as a portfolio of investments, treating each group as distinct entities and handling them in a customised way.

Principle 2: Tiered targets and prizes

Don't just motivate your top performers. Introduce a tiered approach, with aspirational prizes for the Superstars, Foot Soldiers and the Laggards.

Principle 3: Multiple prizes — differentiate, don't downgrade

Offer distinct types of prizes. Avoid creating the impression that the second and third place winners won the consolation prize, a prize that was clearly a downgraded version of the first prize. This allows the winners of the lesser prizes to rationalise that in fact they prefer their prize, increasing the chance that all parties can be happy with their reward.

Principle 4: Setting the pace — getting more from the poorest performers

The longer the gap between what we do and the reward, the weaker the impact of that reward becomes. The time period between bonuses can have a major impact on motivation.

Principle 5: Feeling the heat — social pressure keeps 'em keen

An oversupply of high quality talent tends to have a motivating effect on the whole workforce.

Principle 6: Making the most of your Superstars — don't cap commission

Don't cap sales commission [on profitable sales] if you want to maximise revenue.

Principle 7: Reward overachievement <u>more</u>, not less

Offering an higher rate of commission, for sales above a threshold (for example the sales target) can drive sales overachievement.

Principle 8: Spread the love — multiple winners, everyone wins

There should be at least as many prizes as there are Superstars, increasing the likelihood that a Foot Soldier or Laggard will win a prize, so keeping the pressure on the Superstars to perform.

As 'the eight principles of incentive design' doesn't exactly trip off the tongue (and we never miss the opportunity for a cheesy pun), the eight principles will become the **Motive8 Principles** for the rest of the book.

The ROKET-DS™ Diagnostic incentive design failures

By standing the Motive8 principles on their heads and listing the problems that they fix, we can add eight incentive-related failure modes to the ROKET-DS™ Diagnostic tool:

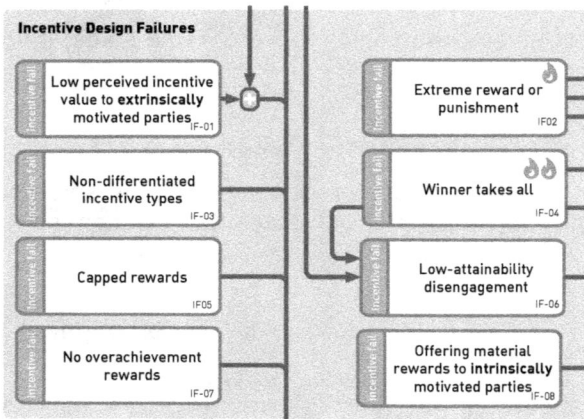

The eight common incentive failure modes

Your guide and memory jogger: The ROKET-DS™ Incentive Canvas

If you have jumped straight to this section, you should know that a pair of useful printable ROKET-DS™ Design Canvases are included in the download pack for this book, one for target design and the second for incentive design. Both are printable sheets, showing each step of the method, some memory jogging crib notes and blank space to populate with your answers.

These canvases can be used together, or individually. The printable PDFs can be found in your download pack. They are best printed out on a big sheet of paper (A3/Tabloid works well, A2 is even better) but there is also a much less pretty but more practical Excel version, with all the fields listed in columns and a blank column to populate.

ROKET-DS®

Incentive Design Canvas

Designed by:		
Target reference:	Incentive reference:	
Date		Version & revision date

10

Draft incentive values & rules
Design incentive
Create 'rules' for incentive

Motive8 Design Principles

Create portfolio incentives
Include more than just top performers in scope

Tier targets and prizes
Don't just motivate your top performers, tiered targets for all

Over supply talent
Social pressure keeps 'em keen

Do not cap commission
Make the most of your Superstars

Differentiate prizes
Differentiate, don't downgrade

Set the pace
Frequent prizes motivate poor performers

Reward overachievement
Overachievement wins more, not less

Create multiple winners
Spread the love, everyone wins

11

White-hat test incentive
How should the incentive work?
Walk through the inputs and outputs of the incentive

12

Black-hat test incentive
Reverse brainstorm how to win incentive in worst-possible way.
Apply **ROKET-DS diagnostic**

Also factor...
- Moral hazard
- Opportunism
- Personal gain optimisation

13

Fix problems & re-test
Put in place mitigations to prevent 'worst possible' behaviours

14

Record & go live with incentive
How will the incentive be launched?
How will incentive designs be stored & shared?
How to manage changes & updates?

ROKET-DS Incentive Canvas Version 1.5 Revised: 19th August 2021

Step 10

Draft incentive values & rules

Step 10: Draft incentives, values and rules

In the first part of the ROKET-DS™ method we designed our targets: our performance thresholds or tiers where good (or bad) things are triggered. In this step we create the first draft of our incentives and the rules associated with those incentives.

What happens in Step 10:

Step 10 is the 'beating heart' of the incentive design process, and also the most demanding step of the ROKET-DS™ Incentive Design process.

This step involves careful thought, some deep discussion, and multiple evolutions of the incentive designs, possibly over a number of sessions.

The inputs to this step are:

- Target values and tiers from Step 9 of your ROKET-DS™ work
- Historic performance data to enable volume projections and costs of incentives to be estimated
- The Motive8 Principles in note form (ROKET-DS™ Incentive Design Canvas), to enable sanity checking of designs
- Details on existing incentives and disincentives in your organisation
- The right stakeholders for development and decision making on incentives

The outputs of the step will be:

- A documented set of draft incentives, with rules
- Supporting notes on how the proposed incentives meet the Motive8 Principles

The Motive8 Principles will provide our regular sanity-check and testbed. Here's a recap of the eight incentive design principles:

1. Use a portfolio management approach — don't just focus on one group
2. Tiered targets and prizes
3. Multiple prizes — differentiate, don't downgrade
4. Setting the pace — getting more from the poorest performers
5. Feeling the heat — social pressure keeps 'em keen
6. Making the most of your Superstars — don't cap commission
7. Reward overachievement more, not less
8. Spread the love — multiple winners, everyone wins

It will normally take a number of attempts before you come up with a set of incentives that satisfies most, or all, of the Motive8 Principles. If you have jumped straight to this section, you can see more on the Motive8 Principles on page 181.

What types of incentive are available?

There are a number of incentive types that we can use. Many of them are extrinsic (external), as we have more control and influence over how these work. Don't forget to think about the impact that these extrinsic rewards may have on a person's intrinsic (internal) motivation. We can end up undermining our own efforts if we accidentally erode a person's intrinsic motivation through the clumsy use of extrinsic rewards (more details on motivation types can be found page 175).

Let's take a look at the types on offer and their pros and cons:

Positive and negative incentives

There are two types of incentives. The first, and most socially acceptable, type are 'positive' or 'reward' incentives. These are offered in exchange for hitting or exceeding set targets.

Positive incentives

It is easy to jump straight to cash as a positive incentive, but other effective alternative options exist. They may seem obvious when listed, but it's worth briskly reviewing the options. Let's take a look at the pros and the cons of each, starting with good old-fashioned money.

Incentive type: Monetary

Achieving a target leads to a monetary reward.

Pros

- Easy to quantify the numerical value of the reward
- Of use to almost everyone

Cons

- Easy to quantify the value of the reward — can lead to devaluation of lower awards
- Can become part of 'expected income' and lose motivational impact
- Because of the importance of money, failure to win can create anger and disengagement in some situations
- Not everyone is motivated by financial reward (which is why we have a galaxy of charities and foundations like Wikipedia in the world)

Incentive type: Recognition

'Recognition' is where a team member's success is <u>publicly</u> acknowledged. This might include 'team member of the month' award, a new job title, personal congratulations from their CEO, or a token 'trophy'.

Pros

- No monetary cost
- Avoids many of the risks of monetary rewards

Cons

- Needs to be delivered with skill and sincerity for maximum effect
- Works better on some personality types than others
- May become devalued through overuse

Incentive type: Experience prize

An experience prize is a reward such as a vacation, tickets to a coveted sports event, or a skydiving course.

Pros

- Easy to differentiate, avoiding devaluation of lesser/ greater prizes
- Avoids the risks of monetary reward
- Effectiveness can be amplified by peer recognition of the desirability of the prize
- May have high benefit-to-cost ratio, when chosen correctly

Cons

- Motivational effect <u>strongly</u> influenced by the personal taste of the recipient
- Can be difficult to choose prizes that are appropriate and motivational to the <u>whole</u> team
- May require complex administration and organisation

Incentive type: Material prize

A material prize is something physical like a case of wine, smartphone, or a juicer.

Pros

- It may be easier to find items with broad appeal than is the case for experience prizes
- It is easier to manage and deliver material prizes than experience prizes

- There is a symbolic element to awarding a material prize that is missing from financial rewards

Cons

- It can be fairly easy to identify the value of the item, leading to unfavourable comparisons between tier prizes
- The motivational value of a prize is highly dependent on the prize and the individual. An iPad may be highly motivating for someone who doesn't have one already, less so for a person who owns a superior model already
- At the 'modest' end of the reward spectrum, material prizes often become a physical symbol of **recognition**, rather than having significant monetary value in their own right

Incentive type: Privilege

A privilege incentive is where a 'right', such as a coveted parking space, flexible working, or a desirable office desk location is awarded for hitting targets.

Pros

- These awards normally carry peer group prestige
- Low or no cost
- Should be applicable and relevant to all team members

Cons

- Effectiveness of motivation from these awards varies by individual
- Generally suitable for modest rewards. Excessive privileges can start to breed team resentment

- There may only be a finite number of privileges that can be awarded

Incentive type: Qualification, badge, or title

A qualification reward is where a team member earns the right to use a title, put on a badge, or a wear a different uniform to show their achievement. Each McDonalds 'crew member' used to have a name badge with up to four gold stars on it, announcing the skills they had acquired. Microsoft awards qualifications and titles such 'Most Valued Professional' — an award made to non-Microsoft employees for their contributions to community. Their website states the MVP award is:

To say thank you to top-notch technology experts who make outstanding contributions to their communities

Pros

- Low or no cost
- Objective, usually based on very clear achievement criteria
- Leverages recognition and peer prestige in delivering reward value

Cons

- Effectiveness of motivation from these awards varies by individual — certain individuals may get little or no motivation from this kind of award

You will notice that every single reward type comes with the disclaimer that this reward type may not work for all team members in their cons list. It is important to remember that individuals can have wildly different drivers. There are two things we can do to manage this:

1. Take time to get to know what makes a team tick. By all means ask the team what incentives they would like, but remember people tend to head straight to 'more money' as a default answer when experience and observation shows that this is often not the best motivational tool. Watch and learn 'what works' too.

2. Don't rely on just one incentive type, use a range of incentives. This reduces the risk of accidentally leaving a portion of the team behind and will give you a testbed for what motivates and what doesn't.

Negative incentives (disincentives)

Disincentives are the mirror of incentives. These are punishments, forfeits, or hardships that are meted out when a target is not met. They create motivation through fear of loss, pain, embarrassment, or reduced status. Disincentives can be highly effective as research shows that fear of loss carries more weight for most people than the opportunity for gain.[24] However, disincentives can also breed misery, dishonesty, and criminal behaviour if they are badly designed or mismanaged. These are the tools of prisons, tax agencies and carpark owners. Use them carefully!

Having said that, it's always useful to know what they look like, so you can make a considered choice.

Most of our disincentives are the 'evil twins' of the positive incentives we have just listed. Please bear in mind that many of these are illegal in normal society, and those which are technically legal are often amoral.

Let's take a look at the rogues' gallery...

Disincentive type: Fines or monetary loss

This type of disincentive is where a team member is fined for failing to achieve a target.

There are some variations on this approach. Tax agencies and car park owners are masters of the clear-as-day fine or penalty. During the payment protection mis-selling scandal in the UK in the 1990s-2010, bank sales people were sometimes paid their bonus 'in advance' and it was reclaimed if they failed to meet their targets. On paper this may not be a 'fine' but in practice it definitely felt like a fine to the staff members. In some organisations, staff may have the opportunity to work overtime withdrawn as a punishment. Again this is not technically a fine, but will have a similar impact.

There are situations where this approach has worked very well. The introduction of a low, five pence charge for single-use shopping bags in the UK led to a 92% reduction in their use over five years (more details on page 247).

Disincentive type: Public humiliation

Publicly declaring an individual or team 'failure' is a common punishment. The media and court records are littered with disgraced individuals. In a business environment public humiliation can be crushingly effective in the short term, but is also very corrosive (aside from being illegal, as a form of bullying). Aside from the personal pain and anguish is inflicts on the victim, it encourages all team members to hide the truth or even lie. Healthy organisations rely on open, honest discussion to function and improve. Destroying team members' desire to be open and honest leads to very dark outcomes for any organisation, be it a corporation, not-for-profit, or government.

Disincentive type: Unpleasant work role or task

Punishment activities are the staple of prisons, armed forces, and boarding schools. They are intended to motivate through the desire to avoid unpleasant, degrading, and socially stigmatised tasks. Whilst fixed-period, specific punishment tasks can be unpleasant and embarrassing, permanent 'punitive roles' can be highly damaging. These 'punishment roles' can not only psychologically damage the recipients, but they can also lead to drastically lower performance. Research shows that performance levels adjust to meet management expectations, dubbed the Pygmalion effect.[25]

Disincentive type: Material forfeit

This form of disincentive is similar to 'fines or monetary loss' but involves the loss of material possessions. Again, a staple of prisons, dictatorships, and governments this creates both a loss of resource and social humiliation. In the UK untaxed cars have been publicly crushed as punishment and to encourage others to pay their vehicle tax.[26]

Disincentive type: Loss of privilege

Potential loss of privilege offers the risk of discomfort and loss of social status. A prisoner may lose their right to have a television in their cells (and risk boredom) or the right to wear their own clothes (loss of comfort and social status).

Disincentive type: Loss of rank, badge, status or title

This disincentive is fairly common in almost all walks of life and across all industries in modern society. The media frequently report soldiers losing rank, clergy being defrocked, doctors being struck off, and directors being barred from company ownership.

Just to repeat myself, I've listed these as a <u>warning</u>. I would advise extreme caution before even thinking about using any of these disincentives as they can create all kinds of unintended negative consequences. They are seductively effective in the short term, but dangerous and difficult to use in the longer term. Think of these as the dark side of 'The Force'.

Gamification

Gamification is the process of using the psychological quirks of human behaviour to increase engagement. By using these techniques, we can get extra 'bang for our buck' from our reward budget.

Variable reward

One highly effective gamification technique, **variable reward**, will give you a taste of that toolkit.

Research has shown that most people will work harder if a reward is uncertain. Say you have a prize with a 50% chance of winning $100 and a 50% chance of winning $200. Experiments have shown that, on average, people will work harder for that uncertain prize of either $100 or $200 than the absolute certainty of winning $150.

Using variable rewards can be a great way of magnifying team interest and engagement without increasing the cost of the reward. In practice, you might apply this by offering a choice of two envelopes to an incentive winner, one with a larger sum, the other with a smaller amount. For zero extra cost this incentive will generate more effort and engagement with the target.

There's much more to gamification than just variable rewards. I have shared this example to make you aware that there is a diverse gamification toolkit available to help magnify the impact of your incentives.

Case study example: Roughshod Repairs Call Centre

Roughshod

Repairs

(Re)introducing Roughshod

If you have jumped straight to his section, allow me introduce our fictional case study organisation, Roughshod Repairs. Roughshod Repairs is run by Ruby Roughshod and specialises in managing warranties, repairs, and recalls for consumer electronics manufacturers. As part of the business, they run a call centre with about 100 seats. We've chosen a call centre as it's a measurement-heavy environment that most of us have some experience of even if it's only as a customer. So, you should have a good intuitive grasp of what they do and also how things can go wrong.

Applying 'Step 10: Draft incentives, values and rules' to Roughshod Repairs

Ruby applies these principles to Roughshod's incentive design. She holds a workshop session with her team and makes sure they have the target design and historic data to hand.

Using a portfolio approach is straightforward as they have already created three performance tiers:

Solid — a hardworking, competent agent should expect to be able to hit this target 4-6 weeks after coming out of training. The 'Solid' award will be weekly and will be:

• Recognition in the shift team meeting
• Free hot drinks for the following week

Good — 30% of agents should be able to achieve this level of performance on a regular basis. 'Good' awards are reviewed monthly and winners receive:

- Recognition in the monthly team performance cascade
- £50 gift voucher
- 'Preferential scheduling' for the following month

Legendary — just 2% of agents are expected to achieve this level in a given quarter. 'Legendary' awards are quarterly and winners receive:

- Preferential parking spot for the next quarter
- 25% pay bonus for the previous quarter
- Personal thank-you coffee with the centre director

The targets required to hit each of these tiers were decided earlier in the process (page 146), and the overall achievement level is determined by <u>lowest</u> achieved KPI target tier over the previous period.

The team then run through the Motive8 principles and notes whether they have met the principle and, if they have not met the principle, the reasons behind not doing so:

Principle 1: Use a portfolio management approach — don't just focus on one group

The award scheme covers all levels from newly trained agents through to superstars, Ruby and her team have already adopted a portfolio approach.

Principle 2: Tiered targets and prizes

Three tiers have been created, with the intention of offering a motivational incentive scheme to every level of agent in the business.

Principle 3: Multiple prizes — differentiate, don't downgrade

Each tier comes with its own reward package, which is not simply a watered down version of the level above or improved version of the level below.

Principle 4: Setting the pace — getting more from the poorest performers

The incentives for the lowest tier — Solid — are awarded on a weekly basis to keep that group fully engaged with the target and incentive scheme.

Principle 5: Feeling the heat — social pressure keeps 'em keen

Ruby and the team feel this is more appropriate for a sales environment and decide not to over-resource, as this will have a negative impact on their service-delivery costs.

Principle 6: Making the most of your Superstars — don't cap commission & Principle 7: Reward overachievement more, not less

Again, both of these principles are aimed at revenue-generating team members. The Roughshod team do not have sales opportunities, they are delivering a contracted service, so this is not appropriate for their team.

Principle 8: Spread the love — multiple winners, everyone wins

All tiers have multiple winners. For the 'Solid' and 'Good' tiers there are no caps on the number of agents who can win those incentives, it is simply based on hitting the required targets.

Practical tips for Step 10

The incentive drafting process is best done through a workshop discussion if there is more than one person involved in the design.

To make the session a success, it is important to:

- Have the right stakeholders in the room — often a subset of the stakeholders identified in Step 3 of the method
- Have the target design work from Part 2 to hand
- Understand the target tiers you have set
- Understand the Motive8 design principles

By the end of the session, you should have a set of incentives and rules that the group feel will deliver the expected motivation and satisfy the Motive8 Principles.

Nudge: Applying this to your incentives

Drawing on the Motive8 principles, now is the time to design your first-draft incentives and rules. Record those first drafts in Box 10 of the ROKET-DS™ Incentive Design Canvas.

Step 11

White hat test
incentives

Step 11: Incentive white hat testing

In this 'incentive white hat testing' step we take just the same approach as we did in Step 6 for target design. The purpose of the step is to understand how the incentives work when everyone behaves as <u>intended</u> and <u>expected</u>.

What happens in Step 11

We ask one simple question:

> What <u>should</u> happen when people display the behaviours we expect and encourage in the context of targets and <u>incentives</u>?

In this step we are not trying to anticipate any problems or issues, we just walk through the expected behaviour. This does not mean we always assume an ideal outcome, just that our system of incentives functions according to the rules and that people behave in the way we anticipated when building the initial target and incentive systems.

White hat testing may be quite dull, just a case of walking through the thought process and logic that we used in the earlier steps. So, there's typically no surprises because we're simply reinforcing what we've already thought of. Sometimes you will pick up some rule and logic issues through talking things through. It's well worth doing, and as was the case for Step 6, it's necessary preparation for the more intriguing black hat testing.

Case study example: Roughshod Repairs Call Centre

Roughshod

Repairs

Ruby and the group walk through the incentive process, assuming that the agents behave as honest actors whose interests are aligned with those of the organisation, and ask, "How does our incentive design work when used <u>as expected</u>?"

- Agents aspire to be fully trained, available, and serve callers swiftly, politely, and compliantly
- Our agents resolve the customer's issues on first touch wherever possible
- Within a few weeks of joining Roughshod, new agents achieve the 'solid' award
- Most agents then go on to achieve 'good' at some point in their career
- The 'legendary' awards keep the best agents in the business and the award acts as an aspiration for our mid-performers

Practical tips for Step 11

Drawing out a simple process flow can help in the walkthrough of the incentive process. A process map can also be a useful tool when explaining the new incentives to the wider team.

Nudge: Applying this to your incentives

It's time to consider how your incentives <u>should</u> work by walking through the inputs and outputs of each incentive. Record the key points of the walkthrough in Box 11 of the ROKET-DS™ Incentive Design Canvas.

Part 3: How to design effective incentives (or fix broken ones)

Step 12

Black hat test incentives

Step 12: Incentive black hat testing

Black hat testing is all about spotting real world, unintended behaviours and consequences linked to our draft incentives before we go live and before we discover those issues in the worst possible way. It is a powerful way of avoiding embarrassing, unintended outcomes, but also helps us develop a set of robust rules for enforcement of our incentives, as we will have a much better understanding of the loopholes, cheats, and shortcuts people might use to win those incentives.

Step 12 is very similar to Step 7, but in this case we are focusing on the unintended behavioural impacts of the incentives, rather than the targets. Let's look at an example of the difference between Steps 7 and 12:

Cheating to hit a target (and win an incentive) should show up in Step 7, whereas avoiding promotion because your current incentive scheme makes you better paid than your boss would show up in Step 12, as it is an issue with the incentive design itself.

If you jumped straight to this section you can find more background on the origins of black hat testing on page 129.

What happens in Step 12

In 'black hat incentive testing' we apply the same tools we used in 'Step 7: Black hat testing': reverse brainstorming the ROKET-DS™ Diagnostic, and the Design-risk Checklist (see the Appendix).

How Reverse Brainstorming works

The approach is based on a very simple idea: asking the people affected by the new targets and incentives,

> *How could the 'right' result be achieved in the stupidest possible way?*

We list all the ways in which things might be corrupted or go wrong, and then identify countermeasures and mitigations. The full approach for running a reverse brainstorming workshop session is detailed on page 131.

ROKET-DS™ Diagnostic

The ROKET-DS™ Diagnostic is a schematic diagram, showing the relationships between common target design issues, incentive design issues, management and behavioural dysfunctions.

It is a powerful tool to extend the reverse brainstorming conversation. It is best used after the initial reverse brainstorm.

Once the initial flush of team ideas has been discussed and recorded, the ROKET-DS™ Diagnostic can be used to prompt further discussion. The diagnostic is shown on page 65 and is also included in your download pack.

The Design Risk Checklist

There are a number of simple questions that can help flush out potential issues, such as:

- What is the impact of the most extreme incentive case(s) in <u>financial</u> terms?

  Example: Might we have a cash flow issue if our sales team rewards massively exceed expectation?

- What is the impact of the most extreme incentive case(s) in <u>operational</u> terms?

  Example: Will our star performer retire if they earn the top end of their rewards package?

- What would be the <u>media impact</u> of the most extreme incentive cases?

  Example: How would a huge CEO bonus figure play with the public and shareholders?

These questions, and a number of others are included in the Design Checklist in the Appendix.

Case study example: Roughshod Repairs Call Centre

Using Reverse Brainstorming and the ROKET-DS™ Diagnostic as a discussion aid, Ruby and the team identify two significant potential issues with the proposed incentives:

- If an agent wins a 25% bonus for achieving 'legendary' performance, an agent will be earning <u>more</u> than their supervisors, so it could be hard for the business to recruit those high performers into team manager roles.

- The Human Resources and Finance heads are nervous about the cost impact of an unexpectedly large number of people winning 'legendary' award status. Remember our agents are not able to 'sell' so whilst their performance is important for contract fulfilment and customer service, they are not able to generate additional profit through the call activities and their income is a 'cost' to Roughshod. All the modelling indicates an expected win rate of 2% of agents, but in our first draft we have not capped that figure, just set a performance threshold. If a higher percentage of the team meet or exceed that threshold, Roughshod could be in for a unexpectedly large payroll bill.

Nudge: Applying this to your incentives

It's time to think about how your incentives will perform in the real world. Use reverse brainstorming and the ROKET-DS™ Diagnostic to work out the worst possible outcomes and log those results in Box 12 of the ROKET-DS™ Incentive Design Canvas.

Step 13

Fix problems
& re-test

———————————————

Step 13: Fix problems and re-test

If we identify any issues with the design of our incentives, this is the point where we work out how to fix them. The fix will typically involve an incentive redesign, clarification of the rules, or extra rules for edge cases and specific situations.

What happens in Step 13

We have five main options when fixing our incentives:

1. Adapt the design of the incentive
2. Replace the incentive with another
3. Change the incentive rules
4. Create incentive rule exceptions, exemptions, or special cases
5. Create extra rules

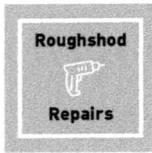

Case study example: Roughshod Repairs Call Centre

Roughshod

Repairs

Taking each of the issues identified by the Roughshod team during black hat incentive testing...

'Legendary' agents earning more than their supervisors.

Recapping on the risk identified in black hat incentive testing...

> *If an agent wins a 25% bonus for achieving 'legendary' performance, an agent will be earning <u>more</u> than their supervisors, so it could be hard for them to recruit those high performers into team manager roles.*

There are a few ways this could be fixed:

1. The agent's bonus could be reduced, to protect the differential.
2. The supervisor's base pay could be increased.
3. The supervisor could receive a reward for having one or more 'Legendary' award winners in their team.

After some discussion, the group decide that maintaining a manager-agent pay differential by rewarding the supervisors for having 'Legendary' team members creates the right behavioural drivers — creating a positive incentive for the team leaders to support their team's skills development. A supervisor will be rewarded on a per agent basis, so more 'Legendary' agents means a higher bonus for the supervisor.

Cost impact of a large number of 'Legendary' award winners.

The other identified risk was the potential unexpected costs of the 'Legendary' awards.

To tackle that concern, the team agree to cap the number of winners to a maximum rate of 2% of the agent population. If more than 2% of the agent population meet or exceed the 'Legendary' award band, the winners will be ranked and the awards will be allocated from the top of the list downwards, until the winning 'places' have been allocated.

We need to be open and honest with the teams when we launch this, explaining the cap, otherwise they may feel like it's a swindle or a con.

This new rule may look like it runs counter to our 'Do not cap commission' and 'Reward overachievement' design principle, but the cap is necessary given that our agents are not salespeople, do not generate fee income and extra performance doesn't result in more revenue to offset that extra award costs. We need to manage the costs and risks.

Nudge: Applying this to your incentives

If you identified issues in black hat testing this is the point when you should develop rule tweaks and mitigations to curb those unintended behaviours and outcomes. Re-test the revised rules and capture those revisions in Box 13 of the ROKET-DS™ Incentive Design Canvas.

Part 3: How to design effective incentives (or fix broken ones)

Step 14

Record &
go live

Step 14: Record and go live with incentives

Our final step is to implement our incentives using good quality launch messaging and communications, and to make sure the system runs smoothly and effectively in everyday use.

What happens in Step 14

To make our incentives successful, we need a solid technical launch, good buy-in from the organisation, and robust systems and processes in place to manage things after launch.

Implementation, launch, and communications don't have to be complicated, but there is a long list of things that must happen to make sure our incentives are successful. Checklists are the tool to help our simple analogue brains handle complex multi-step tasks. That's why we have included the GAMED design and implementation checklists in the Appendix. These checklists help us answer four key questions:

1. How will we <u>communicate</u> the launch and deployment?
2. How will the new targets and incentives be <u>implemented</u>?
3. How will we <u>manage and sustain</u> our new incentives?
4. How will we deal with <u>problems and issues</u>?

It all starts once it's 'done'

The success of your targets and incentives system will be decided by your attention to detail, particularly after launch. Even the best designed incentive systems have teething problems. It is how quickly, openly, and effectively you acknowledge and tackle those issues that will define your success.

Case study example: Roughshod Repairs Call Centre

Roughshod

Repairs

Ruby and the team use the checklists and outline their plan using the four 'Key questions' from earlier.

How will we communicate the launch and deployment?

The team carefully draft three launch documents, designed to explain:

1. Why targets and incentives are being introduced
2. How the targets and incentives will work and the 'rules'
3. Frequently asked questions

These documents form the communications plan. The broad strokes of the communication plan are:

- Updates on the incentive design process as it progresses
- Pre-briefings of the teams, starting one month before it goes live
- Launch briefings, with ad hoc drop-ins from CEO
- Small group post-launch sessions to flush out issues and concerns

How will the new targets and incentives be implemented?

The targets and current progress will be displayed on the call handling system. Roughshod's systems provider has been asked to enable live target performance data on the agent's screens. Team targets and scores will be shown on the large ceiling-mounted screens in the centre.

How will we manage and sustain our new incentives?

The quality manager, Rebecca Righteous, has been given ownership of the targets and incentives system performance. Ownership includes <u>every</u> aspect of the systems, not just the IT and technical aspects. Rebecca has been made directly accountable to the CEO for the robustness and reliability of the management and IT processes that are needed to make the targets and incentives system successful.

As a start, Rebecca creates proper process maps for the target and incentive process. She adds the process maps and maintained definition documents for each target and incentive to the intranet wiki they set up. The definitions on the intranet are based on the fields populated in the ROKET-DS™ Incentives Canvas.

How will we deal with problems and issues?

The wiki and FAQ documents are intended to be the first port of call for anyone with a query. If that doesn't answer the question, then questions or issues need to head to Rebecca first. If the problem turns out to be an issue that isn't covered by the current rules and processes, it then goes to the 'Targets and Incentives Steering Group'. This meets on a monthly basis, but special sessions can be called at short notice, when things are urgent.

The 'Targets and Incentives Steering Group' is also where individual disputes and complaints about targets and incentives are reviewed, using a pre-agreed framework.

Nudge: Applying this to your incentives

It's time to plan your launch, the practicalities of running your incentive scheme and to organise launch communications. Use the GAMED design and implementation checklists to help you do this and record the headlines in Box 14 of the ROKET-DS™ Incentive Design Canvas.

Some words of caution

As with any complex adventure, there are some tricky human behavioural traits that we need to keep an eye on, as unchecked they can quickly destroy our hard work.

Opportunism, the crocodile of the target and incentive world

The first of these behavioural traits is 'opportunism'. If you open the Cambridge English Dictionary it defines opportunism as:

Behaviour in which you use every situation to try to get power or an advantage.

Opportunism is all about <u>self</u>. We designed our targets and systems to harness self-interest, but many behavioural dysfunctions in our diagnostic actually spring directly from opportunism.

If you look at behavioural symptoms on the right-hand side of the ROKET-DS™ Diagnostic [copy available in your free download pack, details in the first section of this book], every dysfunction is rooted in opportunism. Our best tool, when it comes to dealing with opportunism, is not dealing with it at all but instead <u>restraining</u> that opportunism. It is such a deeply ingrained character trait in most humans that it never really goes away so the best we can hope for is to keep it in check as often as possible.

So, our objective when designing an incentive system is to keep opportunism in check and perhaps steer it to become a force for good. Our best tactics for this are:

- Clear rules and guidelines, effective policing of those rules and guidelines, and serious consequences for infringement (i.e., the price of breaking the rules).

A strong feedback loop, making sure you adjust and update the rules based on unanticipated behaviour quickly and transparently, is also essential.

- Strong healthy **social norms**, the powerful unwritten rules present in any organisation. Senior management's behaviour plays a critical part in setting and maintaining those cultural standards.

- Finally, regular well-designed black hat testing will help keep you ahead of the curve in the race to circumvent the spirit and rules of the incentives.

Remember, dealing with opportunism is a little like handling crocodiles, just because the crocodiles look calm and disinterested, don't assume that bad things can't happen very quickly if you stop paying attention. If you don't have an issue with opportunism, don't assume that you never will. Keep an eye on it, it's the thing that breaks and corrupts systems faster than you can say, "Disastrous news headlines".

Moral hazard

The next risk we need to come to grips with is **moral hazard**.

If you're not familiar with this term, imagine the situation. You've got two drivers, the first driver is in a luxury Swedish car, the car has crash prevention, auto emergency braking, intelligent high beam system, lane departure warning, driver sleep detection, and adaptive cruise control. The second car has none of these features, just a single sword blade mounted in the centre of the steering wheel, pointing towards the driver. Which of the drivers will drive more carefully?

You would probably agree that the 'death trap' driver is going to be the more careful of the two. She's likely to adjust her driving style, to accommodate the much higher perceived risk that she faces from the lack of safety features and the danger feature that's built into her car. Moral hazard is the risk that the safe vehicle driver is likely to experience knowing that she is driving a super safe Swedish technical marvel. She's <u>more likely to take risks</u> than the death trap driver, undermining some or all of the benefits of the safer design of vehicle.

Wikipedia puts it concisely: 'Moral hazard occurs when an entity has incentive to increase its exposure to risk, because it does not bear the full cost of that risk.'

Any parent who has replaced their child's broken or lost mobile phone multiple times will instantly understand this concept.

Moral hazard is something we need to think about carefully as we design our targets and incentives. Offering rewards that can be achieved through extreme risk-taking, when the consequences of failure are not felt by the person taking the risks, stokes opportunism and leads to dire outcomes. We see this with the chief executives who hobble their own companies through disruptive cost cutting, only to walk away with fat bonuses, immune from the subsequent collapse in company value, as the effects of their behaviour begin to surface. On the opposite end of the spectrum, we would also see a lack of moral hazard with a salesperson who's paid entirely through a fixed salary. A failure to sell would have no negative impact on their income, so there will be little, if any, extrinsic incentive to sell at all.

Key principle

Introduce some moral hazard into your incentive system, so incentivised individuals are forced to live with the consequences of any opportunism and excessive risk taking.

Opportunity, support and resources

Imagine you run a village football team and you returned to the village having hired the star player from the most recent World Cup winning team. Although your new team will be dramatically improved, it will certainly not win a major championship. Within organisations, like sports teams, stars do not excel in <u>isolation</u>. Their ability to perform is heavily dependent on the people, systems, and resources around them.

A sales team will only thrive if it has:

- A competitive product or service to sell
- Decent pre-sales support
- Credible marketplace reputation
- Acceptable lead times
- After-sales support

If any part of the total offer is weak or absent, then sales performance will be impaired.

So, if you are setting targets and incentives, and want big results, look at the <u>complete system</u> required to deliver the outcome you are looking for rather than just a narrow section of that process.

The motivation conversation

Whilst the ROKET-DS™ process is designed to systematise the process of designing targets and incentives as much as possible, at the heart of things we are dealing with individual human beings.

Every person has different drivers, motives, and quirks. Research will only get us so far, skilled managers will already know that it can be hard to find out what <u>really</u> motivates someone.

How you have the conversation comes down to a number of things, including culture, personality, levels of trust, and time. How ever you do it, you will need to explore:

- The goals of the individual
- The things that person thinks are important: wealth, recognition, status, altruism, virtue, or something else?
- Whether the organisation's and individual's goals align
- Is that person intrinsically motivated, extrinsically motivated, or a combination of the two?
- If they are extrinsically motivated, is it material or social reward that makes them tick?

How significant a motivator is money?

For most extrinsically motived people, monetary reward has its limits. There's been lots of research into the link between **salary** and motivation. A meta-analysis of 120 papers by Tim Judge and his colleagues in Harvard Business Review [27] on this subject, concluded that:

> *...there is a less than 2% overlap between pay and job satisfaction levels.*

And also...

> *...the correlation between pay and pay satisfaction was only marginally higher (r = .22 or 4.8% overlap), indicating that people's satisfaction with their salary is mostly independent of their actual salary.*

Whilst one-off monetary rewards sit in a slightly different category from salary, it is safe to say that what people <u>say</u> motivates them and what <u>really</u> motivates them may well be different. Good observation and testing can often be valuable in this situation.

If in doubt, try it out

If you find yourself struggling to understand what really motivates your team, it's time to do some testing. Try out your rewards in a controlled way. Two key points to keep in mind when you do this are:

1. Rewards may have a temporary effect. Don't get too excited if a new reward has a short-term boost, the effects can often fade. You may need longer-term tests, if you are looking for longer-term motivational tools.

2. Position the tests carefully. Withdrawing a reward can backfire if you have not been very careful to position that reward as temporary or a trial.

You may also consider offering a selection of rewards to every winner, either as a permanent reward strategy or to gather data on the preferred choices.

The impact of culture on behaviour

The term 'culture' can seem hard to pin down. Let's make it simple. When it comes to organisational behaviour, 'culture' means:

- The unwritten rules by which an organisation is run.
- The unstated goals and values which are seen to be important to an organisation.

These 'unofficial' rules and goals are communicated to the team through:

- The decisions, behaviours, actions, rewards, and sanctions of the senior managers in the organisations.

- Deliberate lack of action, wilful ignorance or inaction by those same managers when 'official' rules and values are breached.

A quick look at any news website will reveal large organisations with lofty, moral, and stringent 'official' values, goals, and controls are often caught behaving in a way that seems directly opposed to their officially stated objectives. Cultural rot, an unofficial and unhealthy culture, is at the root of many of the case studies we mentioned earlier.

When it comes to culture, <u>behaviour</u> and <u>actions</u> are king. The unwritten rules and goals signalled by the actions (or inaction) of senior leaders are closely watched and mirrored by their reports.

From a targets and rewards perspective, a healthy culture requires:

- Well-balanced rules, regulations, and commitments that are strictly honoured, particularly when it comes to behaviour.
- The 'price' of cheating, rule bending, or law breaking is made clear and more than offsets the benefit (Moral Hazard, page 230).
- Policing of the systems is effective, transparent, and is not corrupted by a chain of command that has a vested interest in weakening the regulatory system.
- A high standard of expected behaviour from senior managers, with swift and decisive action where they fall short.

Recap: ROKET-DS™ incentive design method

Let's recap and review the five steps of the incentive design process. (Remember the reason we start at Step 10 is because our incentive design method picks up where our target design method finished off, at Step 9):

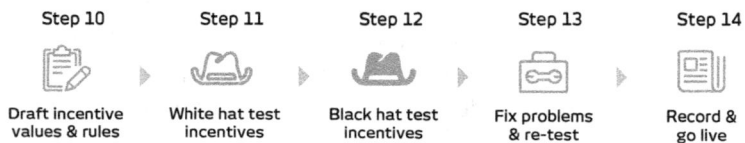

Step 10	Step 11	Step 12	Step 13	Step 14
Draft incentive values & rules	White hat test incentives	Black hat test incentives	Fix problems & re-test	Record & go live

Step 10: Draft incentives, values, and rules

In Step 10 we create the first draft of our incentives and the rules associated with those incentives using the Motive8 Principles:

The Motive8 Principles

Principle 1: Portfolio management — Don't just focus on one group

Within any team there will always be Superstars, Foot Soldiers and Laggards.

Treat your team as a <u>portfolio</u> of investments, treating each group as distinct entities and handling them in a customised way.

Principle 2: Tiered targets and prizes

Don't just motivate your top performers. Introduce a tiered approach, with aspirational prizes for the Superstars, Foot Soldiers and the Laggards.

Principle 3: Multiple prizes — Differentiate, don't downgrade.

Offer <u>distinct</u> prizes. Avoid creating the impression that the second and third place winners won the 'consolation prize', a prize that was clearly a downgraded version of the first prize. This allows the winners of the lesser prizes to rationalise that in fact they prefer their prize, increasing the chance that all parties can be happy with their reward.

Principle 4: Setting the pace — Getting more from the poorest performers

The longer the gap between what we do and the reward, the weaker the impact of that reward.

Principle 5: Feeling the heat — Social pressure keeps 'em keen

An oversupply of high quality talent tends to have a motivating effect on the existing workforce.

Principle 6: Making the most of your Superstars — Don't cap commission

Don't cap sales commission [on profitable sales] if you want to maximise revenue.

Principle 7: Reward overachievement <u>more</u>, not less

Offering a higher rate of commission, for sales above a threshold (for example the sales target) can drive sales over-achievement.

Principle 8: Spread the love — Multiple winners, everyone wins

There should be at least as many prizes as there are Superstars — increasing the likelihood that a Foot Soldier or Laggard will win a prize — so keeping the pressure on the Superstars to perform.

Step 11: Incentive white hat testing

The purpose of this step is to understand how the incentives work when everyone behaves as <u>intended</u> and <u>expected</u>. We ask one simple question, very similar to the one in Step 6, but extended to cover incentive process behaviour too:

What <u>should</u> happen when people display the behaviours we expect and encourage in the context of targets and incentives?

Step 12: Incentive black hat testing

Black hat testing is all about spotting potential real world, unintended behaviours and consequences resulting from our draft incentives <u>before</u> we go live and discover those issues in the worst possible way. Step 12 is very similar to Step 7, but in this case we are focusing on the unintended behavioural impacts of the incentives, rather than the targets. We use reverse brainstorming and the ROKET-DS™ Diagnostic tool to tease out the many ways in which our new incentives could misfire.

Step 13: Fix problems and re-test

If we identify any issues with the design of our incentives, this is the point where we work out how to fix them. The fix will typically involve an incentive redesign, clarification of the rules, or extra rules for edge cases and specific situations.

We have five main options when fixing our incentives:

1. Adapt the design of the incentive
2. Replace the incentive with another
3. Change the incentive rules
4. Create incentive rule exceptions, exemptions, or special cases
5. Create extra rules

Step 14: Record and go live with incentives

Our final step is to implement our incentives using good quality launch messaging and communications, and to make sure the system runs smoothly and effectively in everyday use.

To make our incentives successful, we need a solid technical launch, good buy-in from the organisation, and robust systems and processes in place to manage things after launch.

The key things you need to remember are covered in the GAMED Implementation Checklists in the Appendix. These checklists help us answer four key questions:

1. How will we communicate the launch and deployment?
2. How will the new targets and incentives be implemented?

3. How will we <u>manage and sustain</u> our new incentives?

4. How will we deal with <u>problems and issues</u>?

All five of the incentive design steps are summarised on a single page in the ROKET-DS™ Incentive Design Canvas [copy available in your free download pack, details in the first section of this book]

Part 4: Making it happen

Part 4: Making it happen

Targets and incentives can drive stunning change...

In Part 1 we dissected eight case studies of failure and dysfunction linked to poor target and incentive design. Those eight autopsies helped us understand the many potential maladies and the cure: the ROKET-DS™ approach.

Reviewing so many examples of targets and incentives that backfire, it would be easy to become a little pessimistic. Let's look at a couple of examples to remind ourselves of the awesome power of well-designed and implemented targets and incentives.

Targets: Smallpox, effective targets, and eating a Jeep tyre

Smallpox has stalked humanity for at least 30,000 years. The highly contagious virus kills up to 35% of those who contract it and often leaves the survivors terribly scarred. Smallpox killed at least 300 million people in the 20th century alone.[28] It has been feared throughout history, with good reason.

The very first smallpox vaccine was identified in 1796 by Edward Jenner, when he noticed that people infected with cowpox appeared to be immune to smallpox. Jenner's discovery was followed by the Dryvax vaccine, developed by Wyeth in the late 19th century.

The development of an effective vaccine was a big step forward, but much of the world's population still did not have reliable access to vaccines. Rapid and devastating outbreaks were still a common feature of public health in the more remote and less developed communities around the globe, even with the existence of an effective vaccine.

In 1958, the World Health Organization (WHO) set a target. That target was to eradicate smallpox. Their initial plan was to aim for 100% vaccination. This approach proved successful in eradicating smallpox from Western Europe, North America, Japan, and other areas, but outbreaks remained a feature in more densely populated areas, such as India, even with vaccination rates over 80%. A review of the programmes suggested that mass vaccination alone could not eliminate smallpox in densely populated countries such as Bangladesh, India, Indonesia, and Pakistan[29]. It became clear that simply 'setting a target for 100% vaccination', with inevitable undershoot, was not going to deliver the elimination of smallpox.

A more effective approach was discovered by accident during a 1966 outbreak in Nigeria. Despite over 90% of the population being vaccinated, smallpox got a toehold, originating from a religious community that had resisted vaccination. Vaccine supplies were delayed, so the programme was forced to quickly locate and isolate infected villages so they could target use of their limited vaccine supplies. A reporting network, using radios, was set up to help locate new cases. Teams moved swiftly to isolated infected people and to vaccinate exposed villages.

The surveillance and containment approach worked well and showed an effective method for containing outbreaks even where vaccination levels were below 50%.[30] This approach was progressively refined and tuned using innovations such as smallpox recognition cards, watch guards, rewards for reporting cases, rumour registers, and containment books.

On January 1, 1967, the World Health Organization launched the Intensified Smallpox Eradication Programme using the detection, isolation, and control approach.

Not everyone believed the eradication goal was realistic, or even possible. One WHO official commented that if the India campaign were successful, he would "Eat a tyre off a Jeep"[31]. On the 26th October 1977, the last case of smallpox was reported in Somalia and Donald Henderson, director of the smallpox program, sent that person a Jeep tyre.

The success of the programme hinged on the intelligent selection and use of metrics and targets. Earlier eradication failed because they had confused the means, 100% vaccination, with the end — the eradication of smallpox. By using surveillance, isolation and rapid response, they achieved their goal.

For the first time, a horrific major disease has been completely eradicated. The programme would not have succeeded without impressive technical innovations such as a robust freeze-dried vaccine and the development of the 'bifurcated needle' for easy delivery, but it took more than just clever technical innovations. The Director-General of the World Health Organisation, Dr H. Mahler, described the smallpox programme as "A triumph of management, not of medicine".

A clear focus on the right strategic outcome and the use of effective metrics, targets, and incentives played a major role in that triumph.

Incentives: Can five pence change the world?

Plastic is an amazing material. Strong, cheap, waterproof, and easily shaped into everything from shopping bags to heart valves, it is the wonder material of our age.

Like anything that is cheap, effective, and versatile, there are downsides. Single-use plastic shopping bags are choking the world's oceans. It is estimated that more than 150 million tonnes of plastic waste is drifting in the world's oceans and causing the deaths of a million birds and 100,000 sea mammals each year.[32]

In 2014 over 7.6 billion single-use shopping bags were given to customers by the major UK supermarkets.[33] This is 140 bags per UK resident per year or 60,000 tonnes of plastic waste. In 2015 the UK government decided to take action on single-use plastic shopping bags.

Their plan was to introduce a minor disincentive for the distribution of single-use plastic bags, a five UK pence (7 US cents) customer charge per bag. On October 15th 2015 a new law was introduced, requiring shops to charge for single-use bags.

The impact of this minor disincentive was immediate, dramatic, and sustained. There were some unexpected wrinkles, such as the increase in the sales of heavier 'bags for life', but the net effect was strongly positive. By 2019–2020 supermarket single-use bag sales had dropped to 564 million bags, a decrease of 7 billion bags compared with 2014, or a 92% reduction.

This law alone will not fix the issue of plastic waste and pollution, but it does show the power and positive impact of a well-designed incentive.

Creating <u>your</u> success story

For all the power and sophistication of the ROKET-DS™ approach, there is one thing that is certain to make it fail: <u>not applying it</u>.

The behaviour and motivations of humans can never be reduced to a simple equation or set of rules. People, and the organisations they build, are complex, messy, and in constant flux.

There is no 'magic wand' for creating reliable, robust targets and incentives, but the ROKET-DS™ approach does offer a transparent method for systematically designing, reviewing, and testing all the moving parts of our target and incentive designs, giving you a far better chance of success than any other approach.

Getting going

There are four things you can do to increase your chances of turning your objectives into real-world results using ROKET-DS™...

1. Target something that REALLY counts

The ROKET-DS™ is not a quick-fix solution. You will need to invest time and effort into making it work. Pick an aspect of your organisation that really justifies that commitment and will repay your effort many times over.

2. Don't do it on your own

Plenty of psychological research shows that commitments are much more likely to be followed-through if a person makes their goal publicly known. The ROKET-DS™ method is designed to be a tool that can be used by teams, so making a public declaration of target-design-intent upfront will stiffen your resolve and prime your team for their involvement.

3. Make a plan

If you are a seasoned manager or project manager, you are probably rolling your eyes at this step being spelled out. ROKET-DS™ is a <u>multi-step</u> process, so having a plan, with activity timing estimates, resource plans, and perhaps governance (for larger projects) will increase your chance of success.

4. Ask for help if you need it

If you find yourself stuck, confused, or stalled as you develop your targets and incentives head to...

madetomeasurekpis.com

...for additional resources and materials on ROKET-DS™, building KPI Trees and many other performance management techniques. If you need more hands-on help, or want to talk, drop an email to...

gamed@madetomeasurekpis.com

...and we will help you find the support you need.

Getting support

This book is designed to give you everything you need to implement the ROKET-DS™ approach. Not everyone has the time, bandwidth, or inclination to make the journey on their own.

If you would like to take things further, register for the download pack at **bettertargets.info** (using the password **GAMED888**) and look out for the welcome email with details on how to...

- Join the GAMED Community to access bonus materials, ask questions and take part in discussions
- Sign up for the GAMED online course at a discounted rate
- Arrange one-to-one support, consulting, or in-house training

If you are in a hurry for live help, just send an email to **info@madetomeasurekpis.com** to set up a call.

Simple isn't always easy

I spent the first few years of my career solving industrial problems for a living.

I was regularly called into large manufacturing organisations that were in deep distress: losses running at millions of dollars a day, legal jeopardy, and customers leaving for other suppliers. My work would involve days, sometimes weeks, patiently observing complex industrial processes, manually gathering data, and applying rigorous structured problem solving.

The root cause of those process problems were often a handful of simple-sounding issues: a notched O-ring, a shortage of anti-caking agent, or perhaps an incorrect tension setting. The fix was often deceptively straight-forward and had dramatic positive results. The process of finding that solution was <u>not</u>.

Setting winning targets and motivating incentives can be a similar journey. The final result of the ROKET-DS™ design process may look deceptively simple, perhaps even inevitable. It may be tempting to take a few shortcuts. <u>Don't be fooled</u>. The success or failure of your targets and incentive lies in your hands, and depends on you rigorously following a structured and logical method.

Great results do not happen by accident. The ROKET-DS™ method gives you a ground-breaking end-to-end design process for designing targets and incentives that work in the real world. Now you have that 'secret weapon' at your fingertips I hope you use it to create your own story of 'inevitable' success.

Good luck!

Bernie

Have you enjoyed this book?

Thanks for buying this book. I hope you found it helpful and relevant to your target and incentive work. I'd love to hear how you have applied the ROKET-DS approach, stories you would like to share or feedback you may have – you can email me on **bernie@madetomeasurekpis.com**. I read every email and promise a reply to any questions.

Online reviews make a huge difference to independent creators like me. If you found this book helpful and relevant could I ask you to take a couple of minutes to leave an honest review on Amazon, or wherever you bought this book? It would make a huge difference.

Thanks!

Bernie

Appendix

Appendix

GAMED

Target and incentive failure types

TF-01: All or nothing

Description

There is a single tier. You either achieve the target or you do not.

Why this is a problem

A target will only act as a motivator if an individual feels they are close enough for it to be a real prospect. In any organisation there will be a spread of performers. Having an 'all or nothing' target means that a substantial part of any population will have no prospect of winning.

If the person is close to winning, the opposite problem may occur, creating extreme motivation and increasing the risk of rule bending, breaking, or law-breaking.

Example

Research by Michael Ahearne, working with a US financial services firm, showed that having multiple levels of targets significantly improved the performance of 'core (middle) performers' within an organisation, with core performers showing a significant uplift from the use of three target tiers, compared with one or two tiers.

TF-02: Incomplete rule definition

Description

The rules for a target do not fully cover all situations.

Why this is a problem

When rules are not complete, it is possible to <u>game</u> the targets to win without delivering the intended positive outcomes.

Example

During the Covid-19 pandemic, the UK government promised '100,000 tests per day'. In an attempt to hit this target, the government changed the calculation method to be based on the number of test kits <u>dispatched</u>, rather than <u>used</u>. This was followed by reports that requests for test kits were supplied with triple the requested quantity, moving the government towards the 100k target without a meaningful real-world benefit.

TF-03: Design input bias

Description

Certain inputs are excluded, by design, to improve the reported results.

Why this is a problem

The measures used to assess whether the target has been hit will be misleading, leading to a situation where a target may be hit and an incentive given, when the real-world performance does not justify it.

Example

In the UK, in some schools it is not uncommon to prevent 'A-level' students from sitting public exams if they are expected to perform poorly or fail. Using this kind of design input bias, schools are able to protect or maximise their average grade performance.

TF-04: Excessively high bar

Description

A target is set at an unrealistically <u>high</u> level.

Why this is a problem

This situation can lead to rapid disengagement from the target recipients or to rule/law breaking.

Example

When a leading UK supermarket, Tesco, set aggressive 2014 profit targets, a whistle-blower described how the senior management team viewed those targets as 'insurmountable'[34]. This perception may have led to the company being forced to admit deliberately overestimating annual profits by £250 million.

TF-05: Intentionally low bar

Description

The threshold is set to an unrealistically <u>low</u> level.

Why this is a problem

A deliberately low target threshold can lead to a reduction in real-world performance, as the target is 'too easy' and does not require high performance levels to meet or exceed it.

Example

Exam 'grade inflation', where the proportion of students achieving top grades increases over time, is thought to be driven by the competitive pressures on examination boards. Put simply, easier curricula and examinations attract the custom of more schools — creating a sustained incentive to 'lower the bar' when it comes to exam difficulty.

TF-06: Weak/no link to intended positive outcome

Description

There is no obvious connection between the targeted KPI and the intended outcome.

Why this is a problem

When there is no clear link between the target and positive outcomes, it can quickly lead to cynicism, frustration, and disengagement.

Example

In the UK ambulance service, for over 40 years an 'A8' target was used for the most serious calls. The target was that 75% of 'life threatening' calls be attended within 8 minutes. There was no medical basis for the 8-minute target, but plenty of pressure to achieve that target on a regular basis, leading to high levels of cynicism and disillusionment amongst those tasked with hitting that target.

TF-07: Arbitrary target selection

Description

There is no obvious connection between the KPI target value and the intended outcome.

Why this is a problem

Arbitrary target selection can lead to cynicism, frustration, and disengagement.

Example

At the core of the Wells Fargo banking scandal was the 'Going for Gr-eight' target. The goal was to cross-sell eight products to every customer. When the architect of this target, CEO Dick Kovacevich, was asked how he came up with the target of cross-selling eight products, his reply was 'It rhymes with GREAT!'[35]

TF-08: Individual and organisational success not aligned

Description

The target set for an individual will not drive outcomes that are beneficial for the organisation.

Why this is a problem

Targets that only benefit the target-recipient will fail to move the organisation towards their intended objectives. In the worst situation the cost of rewards offered to individuals, combined with a lack of tangible benefit, can fatally damage an organisation.

Example

Incentivising computer programmers based on maximising lines of code written can lead to inefficient and difficult to maintain computer code. The coder can hit the target, but the resulting software may not deliver the best outcome for the organisation using it.

TF-09: Lack of pace-setting targets

Description

The interval between target reviews is too long, leading to a loss of motivation.

Why this is a problem

Research shows that weaker performers see an increase in performance from more frequent target-incentive reviews. By not using pace-setting targets we sacrifice the potential benefit.

Example

Elite long-distance runners have long known that it is no good waiting until the end of a race to find out if they were running at the best pace. Lap times, pace calculators, and constant feedback are essential to achieving their best performance. The same applies to any human endeavour. Prompt, accurate, and frequent feedback on performance consistently delivers higher levels of performance.

TF-10: Inappropriate timescale

Description

The target review frequency is not appropriate to influence and control the thing being measured.

Why this is a problem

A long review interval, say an annual review, for a time-sensitive activity (for example customer interaction skills) reduces the benefit from the target-incentive approach, as it breaks the feedback-response loop.

Example

In the UK, state schools receive a government quality assessment called an 'Ofsted rating'. These assessments can have a significant impact on parents' choice of schools. The Ofsted assessment frequency is approximately 4 years. Much can change in 4 years, including the leadership and teaching staff. Choosing a school based on a 4-year-old rating could be compared to driving your car based on what you were seeing 10 minutes ago.

MF-01: Weak enforcement

Description

Target and incentive rules are not enforced rigorously or at all.

Why this is a problem

Weak enforcement undermines the entire measurement-reward system, increasing the chance of cheating, rule breaking, and law breaking. In extreme cases lack of enforcement can lead to complete system breakdown.

Example

In the US Airforce, nine officers in 'leadership positions' in the US Nuclear Missile Program were fired after the discovery of systemic cheating in proficiency exams. They were found to have 'failed to provide adequate oversight' according to Air Force Secretary Deborah Lee James[36].

It is worth noting that the driver behind the cheating seems to have been "Leadership's focus on perfection" which "led commanders to micromanage their people", and pressure to achieve 100% in the exams, despite the pass mark being 90%.

MF-02: Negative leadership behaviour role-modelling

Description

Leadership display behaviours that are not aligned with the rule or spirit of our targets and incentives system.

Why this is a problem

Individuals within an organisation are strongly influenced by non-verbal cues. A leader who breaks rules, games the system, or fails to endorse rule-compliant behaviour can rapidly undermine the system and encourage poor behaviours and outcomes.

Example

In a Vanity Fair article on May 31st, 2017, Bethany McClean relays the words of Yesenia Guitron, a Wells Fargo personal banker:

> "I have come across instances where I've opened accounts and shortly after they are closed and new sets of accounts are opened," she wrote. "I find NO banker notes to explain why this is happening. I am very concerned as I know this to be GAMING!!!" She collected approximately 300 printouts of accounts that were problematic in various ways, she says, such as a minor having more than a dozen accounts. But, according to Guitron in legal documents, her manager would say only, "It's a misunderstanding." Or "You need to mind your own business."

MF-03: Intense management pressure

Description

Intense management pressure is where managers make it clear that targets must be achieved, using a combination of intense scrutiny, praise, threats, or bullying.

Why this is a problem

Managers have multiple ways in which they can apply high levels of pressure to their reports. This pressure can act as an 'accelerant', substantially increasing the likelihood of other negative behaviours and outcomes, such as rule or law breaking.

Example

In Wells Fargo, Shelly Freeman, who ran the Los Angeles region until 2009 then the Florida region, allegedly had district managers 'run the gauntlet'[37] . This involved dressing in a themed costume and running down a line to a whiteboard to report their sales numbers. During the period Q2 2007 to Q4 2012 sales-practice misconduct increased three-fold.

IF-01: Low perceived incentive value to extrinsically motivated parties

Description

A person is motivated by external reward, but the incentive rewards on offer are not sufficiently motivating.

Why this is a problem

If an extrinsically motivated person is offered a reward below their expectation for hitting a given target, then a partial or complete loss of motivation can be expected.

Example

In a manufacturing business, which the author worked with in the 1990s, the factory bonus was set so low that one of the workforce painted the words 'bonus shifter' on the side of a wheelbarrow and left it in a prominent position on the shop floor. Clearly the bonus did not have the motivational impact intended.

IF-02: Extreme reward or punishment

Description

Where the external [extrinsic] reward is of huge importance to the person targeted. Prison, death, or public humiliation are examples of extreme punishment. Extreme rewards might include significant wealth, a major sporting title, or a prestigious job.

Why this is a problem

When extreme rewards or punishments are offered, it can drive extreme, dangerous, or illegal behaviour in an attempt to achieve/avoid that incentive.

Example

Successful sales professionals are often motivated by reward, but at the other end of the performance spectrum, those showing poor performance often have a justified fear of being fired. Fear of job loss often drives extreme behaviours such as selling to customers that they know will not be able to pay, will return the product, or will not yield a profit.

IF-03: Non-differentiated incentive types

Description

Where graded rewards are used (1st place, 2nd place etc.) making the lesser prizes an <u>inferior</u> version of the first prize is an example of 'non-differentiated incentives', lessening the motivational effect of the consolation prizes.

Why this is a problem

If a lower-tier prize is seen as simply an inferior version of the main prize it removes the ability of the winner to rationalise that they 'preferred the prize they won anyway', reducing the motivational power of that prize.

Example

A non-differentiated set of prizes is...

- 1st prize: 5 days in a star Hawaiian 5-star boutique hotel
- 2nd prize: 4 days in a 4-star national hotel chain
- 3rd prize: 3 days in a 3-star national hotel chain

A set of differentiated prizes would be...

- 1st prize: 5 days in a star Hawaiian 5-star boutique hotel
- 2nd prize: A weekend for 2 at a PGA golf resort
- 3rd prize: A supercar track experience

IF-04: Winner takes all

Description

A single winner, with no reward for anyone else, is 'winner takes all'.

Why this is a problem

A 'winner takes all prize' will normally only motivate a small section of the population, those who think they have a reasonable chance of winning that prize, with no motivating effect on the remaining majority.

Example

Many elite sports competitions, such as the World Cup or the Tour de France, are 'winner takes all', at least in terms of prestige and recognition.

IF-05: Capped rewards

Description

A capped reward is where there is a ceiling, or maximum, on the reward that can be won for an open-ended task (e.g., sales). Past the upper limit there is no further reward.

Why this is a problem

A capped reward completely removes any incentive to do more once that cap has been hit. Studies show that a capped reward will have a reduced performance benefit compared with an uncapped reward.

Example

An extrinsically motivated salesman is one that is motivated by external reward. Assuming that external reward has driven them to achieve their sales target, it is not unreasonable to assume that once they achieve their target and no extra reward is available, their motivation will be capped too.

IF-06: Low-attainability driven disengagement

Description

When a target is regarded as 'unattainable' by the recipient (regardless of whether it really is unattainable or not) it can lead to disengagement.

Why this is a problem

A target will only motivate if an individual has some belief that they can reach it. If there is no belief that a target is achievable then it will have no motivational benefits.

Example

This direct quote, from an employee review of their employer summarises the impact of 'unattainable' targets:

> The people you work with are great people. However you're expected to achieve unrealistic targets every day, which is highly demoralising. If the company asked you to try and reach a realistic number, people would be motivated to work hard. Instead they constantly put pressure on you to reach a target which can only be achievable if every email is a simple case that can be resolved in a few minutes, most are not this easy. Management need to realise these targets are doing more harm than good if they want a company people want to work for.

IF-07: No over-achievement rewards

Description

The 'no over-achievement reward' failure is where a high performer exceeds their targets but the incentive scheme does not reflect this over-performance though an increased reward rate.

Why this is a problem

Studies have shown that offering a (progressively) increased reward when an individual exceeds their targets will lead to 17% higher levels of performance. In not offering over-achievement rewards we miss this opportunity. [ref. Thomas Steenburgh]

Example

One practical use of an over-achievement reward would be when selling a house. Offering the estate agent/realtor a very high commission rate for any sales price premium they achieve, perhaps anything above 105% of the current market rate for a property, will give you a good chance of outperforming the market average price. In this situation, you offer the sales professional a generous slice of revenue they might not otherwise realise. It is low risk to the seller and beneficial to both parties to be generous with the commission on the 'surplus' sales revenue. Of course, you should agree this type of deal after the salesperson has valued the property and do a separate market check to avoid the sales agent 'gaming' the expected market price and commission.

IF-08: Offering material rewards to intrinsically motivated parties

Description

Where a person is driven by intrinsic motivation, such as satisfaction or altruism, but is offered external [extrinsic] reward.

Why this is a problem

Offering extrinsic rewards to intrinsically motivated individuals (for example charity volunteers) has been shown to reduce levels of performance in those intrinsically motivated individuals.

Example

A study of Swiss volunteers by Frey, Bruno, Götte, and Lorenz found that offering a small financial reward to volunteers <u>decreased</u> the number of hours they worked, compared with those offered no financial reward.

DB-01: Invisible bar-lowering

Description

The standards required to hit a target are lowered in a non-transparent way.

Why this is a problem

Lowering standards can reduce the credibility of the targets, increase reward costs, and lead to avoidable target boundary revisions.

Example

In manufacturing OEE is a common efficiency measure. Through the measure, we calculate losses due to 'downtime' (machines stopping, a highly visible loss), 'waste' (materials which end up in the waste bin, rather than as good quality finished product) and 'speed' (where the process is running below its ideal speed). As running slowly often reduces the level of 'downtime' (unplanned stops) it is common to quietly reduce the target for speed to improve 'downtime'. Doing this will give us much higher 'efficiency' percentages but will conceal the real opportunity to increase process speed, output, and profitability.

DB-02: Breaking the law

Description

Target-recipients break one or more laws in an attempt to hit their targets.

Why this is a problem

Breaking the law can lead to reputational damage, fines, imprisonment, and company closures.

Example

Volkswagen Audi Group were found to have deliberately manipulated emissions test performance in their vehicles in order to pass US emissions targets without delivering similar emissions performance in real-world usage. This led to a lengthy prison sentence for one executive, costs estimated at $33.3 billion, and a 24% drop in sales.

DB-03: Rule bending or breaking

Description

Target and incentive rules are either subtly or blatantly broken.

Why this is a problem

Rule bending or breaking can lead to demotivation (amongst rule-followers), devaluation of rewards, increased reward costs, reputational damage, and eventually incentive-system collapse.

Example

Staff at a privately-run UK emergency call handling centre were suspended after using their breaks to make and answer fake emergency calls to help them hit their 'Grade of Service' targets.

DB-04: Using loopholes

Description

Behaviour which may <u>technically</u> conform to the rules, but ignores the spirit and intent of those rules.

Why this is a problem

Use of loopholes can reduce confidence in the system, lead to disengagement, and drive perverse behaviours that are not aligned with the intended high-level outcomes.

Example

Sales professionals are particularly good at discovering loopholes. A common loophole is where sales targets do not take into account sales returns. An unscrupulous salesman may ask a customer to place an order on the understanding that it can be returned and the order cancelled as soon as the salesman has hit their sales target.

DB-05: User input misclassification

Description

The users, or administrators of performance measures, targets, or incentives misclassify the input data to gain a performance advantage.

Why this is a problem

User input misclassification can lead to unintended adverse outcomes (e.g., customer dissatisfaction), higher reward costs and frustration from rule-following participants.

Example

Police forces are under intense pressure to maximise their 'clear-up rate', which can drive input classification dysfunctions. The Greater Manchester Police, a UK police force with over six thousand police officers, was found to have closed and (incorrectly) failed to record 80,000 reported crimes a year in June 2020.

DB-06: Unexpected adverse outcomes

Description

Unexpected adverse things happen as a result of achieving or exceeding a target.

Why this is a problem

Targets and incentives are always intended to deliver positive high-level outcomes. Where a target-incentive system has been poorly designed and delivers unexpected adverse outcomes, the system has failed in its single intended purpose.

Example

When attendance targets were introduced in UK schools, they were expected to improve attendance. Under the measure definition, school closures were excluded from the attendance calculation. As a result, when bad weather was anticipated, which might lead to below-target attendance, head teachers were incentivised to close the whole school to protect their attendance figures, as that day would then be excluded from the attendance data set.

DB-07: Output misclassification

Description

A process is misused, by producing an incorrect output/result to achieve a target or win an incentive.

Why this is a problem

Output misclassification can lead to unintended adverse outcomes (e.g., customer dissatisfaction), higher reward costs, and frustration from rule-following participants.

Example

Staff in a major medical insurance claims handling centre determined whether to approve or reject claims. Rejecting claims required lengthy documentation and explanation, approving claims did not. The claims handling team were targeted, and rewarded with bonuses, based on the number of claims they dealt with. Faced with a time-consuming rejection process, many handlers chose to approve claims that were found later to be invalid.

DB-08: Corrupted reporting

Description

Where a correct result is produced by the process but is incorrectly reported to achieve a target or win an incentive.

Why this is a problem

Corrupted reporting can lead to unintended adverse outcomes (e.g., customer dissatisfaction), higher reward costs and frustration from rule-following participants.

Example

In Sicily, during the Covid-19 outbreak of 2020-21, the region's health councillor, Ruggero Razza, was put under house arrest after allegations of altering the number of coronavirus deaths and intensive care admissions in order to avoid being put in the highly restrictive high-risk 'red zone' category.

DB-09: Resource fire-hosing

Description

Excessive levels of resources are dedicated to achieving a target.

Why this is a problem

Whilst resource fire-hosing always makes sense when it comes to 'hitting a target' it can lead to ineffective application of resources when gauged against real-world outcomes. We squander too many resources hitting a target, and we cannot then use those resources more meaningfully.

Example

For serious emergency calls that were likely to be close to the response time target of 8 minutes, the UK ambulance service would sometime dispatch up to four ambulances in an attempt to ensure the incident was attended inside the 8 minute target.

DB-10: Apathy, cynicism

Description

There is significant disengagement as a result of mistrust in the motives, intent, or integrity of targets.

Why this is a problem

Apathy and cynicism are extreme forms of disengagement. They represent a partial or complete loss of motivation and will render that target-incentive system ineffective. These mindsets can also be socially infectious, leading to demotivation and apathy spreading, if not addressed.

Example

In the UK ambulance service, a set of arbitrary response targets for serious emergency calls, collectively known as ORCON were in use for 43 years. The staff of the service recognised the flaws, limitations, and contradictions these targets created. The cynicism this created is clearly summarised in this quote, from a former ambulance paramedic...

> We are hideously overused and understaffed, we face delays at hospital owing to overcrowding and delays on-scene because of the ignorant people we have to attend to. None of this matters – all that matters is the 8 minute deadline. If we make 75% of all calls in 8 minutes we get more money from the government, which means more staff, vehicles that work etc.

Reynolds, Tom. Blood, Sweat and Tea , HarperCollins

DB-11: Loss of intrinsic motivation

Description

Where an individual, previously motivated by internal [intrinsic] factors, such as curiosity, satisfaction, or altruism, loses that motivation.

Why this is a problem

The erosion or destruction of intrinsic (internal) motivation results in lower performance levels.

Example

If you lose interest in a hobby, sport, or activity that once gave you pleasure or satisfaction, that is a loss of intrinsic motivation.

DB-12: Loss of extrinsic motivation

Description

An individual, previously motivated by external [extrinsic] factors, such as the desire to be wealthy, gain status, or avoid punishment, loses that motivation.

Why this is a problem

A loss of extrinsic (external) motivation renders a target-reward system ineffective and results in lower performance.

Example

If you reward your child for tidying their room with a $2 incentive, you may find the incentive succeeds in getting a rapid response the first few times. After a number of repetitions, 'the diminishing effect of rewards' may come in to play, a situation where the payment is 'expected' rather than 'motivating', leading to the partial or complete loss of extrinsic motivation.

Appendix: Failure types

GAMED

Communications planning checklists

Communications message, purpose, and audience

- Why are you communicating?
- What is it that you are trying to change through your communications?
- If you succeed with your communications, do you know what would be different?
- Is that difference quantifiable?
- Do you understand what your target audience currently thinks? If not, you may need to survey them so you can measure any change resulting from the communication.
- If you do know the current audience's view, make sure it is documented properly and can be referred back to after the delivery of the communications plan.
- Who do you need to communicate with? Use the RACI matrix approach to segment your audience.
- Write your key messages for each audience segment — keeping the purpose in mind.

Designing communications activities

- Delivery method — Will it be face-to-face, by email, intranet or teleconference?
- Timing — When will you communicate? How many updates or reminders will they receive?
- Owner — Who will deliver the communications? Will they be trained? Are they suitable and motivated?
- Audience — Are you completely clear about who is included in the communications and what type of communications they will receive?
- Target outcomes from communications — What do you want the audience to know, think, or do as a result of the communications?

Deliver your communications

- Who will deliver the message?
- What preparation do they need?
- Have you drafted 'frequently asked questions and responses' and other backup resources for your deliverers?
- How many people will you need to ensure you cover all the target audience?
- What other resources do you need? e.g., company intranet pages, dedicated SharePoint sites etc.
- How can your audience feed back comments and questions?
- What checks do you have in place to make sure the plan is delivered as intended?
- How can you tell if the communication has been effective?
- How will you know if further communication, over and above the plan, is needed?

Get the message and delivery right

- The depth and method of delivery will be determined by:
- The time available
- The number of people to be engaged
- The geographical distribution of those people
- The communications resources available — especially people to present road shows etc.
- The level of controversy/complexity in the message
- The ability/existing knowledge of the audience

Key communications principles

- Use targeting to make sure you don't unintentionally encourage people to ignore your communications.
- Put yourself 'in the shoes' of your audience. Look at things from their perspective and try to provide them with what they need to know.
- Senior endorsement can help make sure people take the message seriously, even better if the keynote communications are delivered by a senior executive.
- Be as honest as you can be.
- If you expect a bumpy ride, try and have one-to-ones with key players in advance of any group sessions to prevent the sessions becoming 'gladiatorial'.
- Accept that you will not always have the right information to hand. If you don't, commit to getting an answer and do so in the promised timescale.
- Be very, very familiar with the message.

GAMED

Full ROKET-DS process graphic

Target Design

Step 0	Step 1	Step 2	Step 3	Step 4
Identify existing issues	Plan outcome	Match KPIs	Identify & engage target owners	Check owner agency

Step 5	Step 6	Step 7	Step 8	Step 9
Draft target values & rules	White hat test targets	Black hat test targets	Fix problems & re-test	Record & go live

Incentive Design

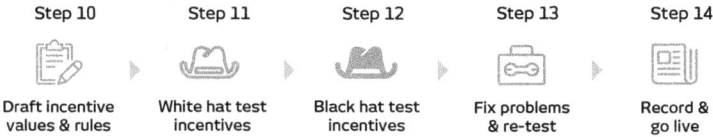

Step 10	Step 11	Step 12	Step 13	Step 14
Draft incentive values & rules	White hat test incentives	Black hat test incentives	Fix problems & re-test	Record & go live

Appendix: Full process

GAMED

Design Checklists: Design-risk

Financial and operational risk

- Identify and assess impact of the most extreme incentive case(s) in financial terms
- Identify and assess the costs and cost-impact for the most likely outcome
- Identify and assess impact of the most extreme incentive case(s) in operational terms (e.g., 'Will our star performer retire?')

Reputational risk

- Identify and assess impact of the most extreme incentive case(s) on morale of the 'winners' and 'losers'
- Assess media impact of the most extreme incentive cases (e.g., huge CEO bonus)
- Identify and assess impact of the most extreme incentive case(s) in social & reputational terms

Legal risk

- Has a legal risk assessment been done on the proposed targets/incentives?
- For multinational organisations, are the proposals legal in all jurisdictions?

Risk mitigation

- Review risk mitigation options such as rule changes or insurance to protect the organisation against extreme cases

Appendix: Design and implementation checklists

Implementation Checklists

Implementation management structure

- Identify steering meeting members
- Set meeting schedule
- Create steering meeting 'Terms of Reference'
- Assign budget
- Create, use, and maintain action lists
- Issue implementation meeting invitations including the following details as a minimum:
  - » Venue
  - » Timing
  - » Agenda
  - » Actions from previous session

Target/incentive management system design

- Identify system owners and managers
- Identify performance owners and managers
- Decide how target and incentive values will be reviewed and how the outcomes will be recorded
- Decide how to manage and maintain revisions and versions of targets and incentives
- Agree how to ensure there is no confusion about current values

Results distribution

- Decide if target/incentive outcomes will be public, shared with a limited audience, or private
- Decide on the process and mechanism for sharing the details of specific targets, incentives, and rules

- Review privacy/data protection considerations
- Are there legal privacy constraints?
- Are there industrial relations risks to consider?
- What is the media risk involved in event of leaks?

Rule design and enforcement

- Design, test, and record system rules for targets and incentives (from Steps 5 and 10 of ROKET-DS™)
- How will we handle rule breaking?
- How will we handle rule bending?
- Clearly designate rules 'police' and build RACI
- What is the process for revising rules?
- Design and enforce a rules communication plan with confirmed-sign-off from target and incentive users

Dispute management

- Decide and agree the process for disputed target or incentive values and goals
- Include the dispute resolution process in the communications plan

Integration of targets/incentives into existing systems

- Document the new processes formally in appropriate process tooling
- Plan any integration into payroll/HR systems
- Plan any integration into reporting/dashboard systems
- Plan any integration into personal scorecards

Rollout: Communications planning

Preparing pre-launch communications

- Identify organisational issues and sensitivities
- Design messaging. Explain...

  - » Why targets and incentives are being introduced/ revised
  - » Who target and incentives apply to
  - » How targets and incentives are calculated
  - » The frequency of reporting and review for targets and incentives
  - » Review process and key dates
  - » How to ask questions or find out more (reference the FAQ resource, if implemented)

- Test messaging in small groups, if needed
- Sign off messaging by appropriate approver

Finalising stakeholder communications list

- Use the **Engage** list from ROKET-DS™ Step 3 as a starting point
- Identify anyone else who needs to know about the new targets and incentives
- Classify stakeholders by role type (taker, setter, enforcer, spectator, customer)

Creating FAQ for rollout communications

- Decide on FAQ medium (email, microsite, wiki etc.)
- Assign ownership of FAQ
- Create initial FAQ document

- Test initial FAQs in focus group
- Maintain and update FAQ
- Agree takedown date, if fixed life

Agreeing approval gates and ownership for communications plan

- Agree communications approval gates dates and formats
- Schedule review and sign-off sessions
- Action any changes or corrections from approval reviews
- Revision review, if required
- Sign-off communications plan

Creating a communications calendar

- Agree delivery medium (email/video call/face-to-face)
- Engage senior stakeholders for messaging design
- Design the communications
- Quality check the draft messages
- Populate the communications schedule
- Deliver the communications in line with the plan
- Collate and review any feedback

Common problems

Team tension and conflict

Symptoms

- Team members sabotage each other to 'win'
- Working relationships break down

Mitigation

- Revisit <u>design</u> of targets and incentives, increasing focus on **collective** outcomes

Unrewarded tasks are ignored

Symptoms

- Work that is important, but not targeted, goes undone
- Team members do not cooperate
- Team members duck responsibilities that are not targeted

Mitigation

- Rebalance target and incentive design to include 'neglected' tasks and outcomes

Rules bent or broken

Symptoms

- Rules are tested to their limit, with loopholes and gaps being exploited in unintended ways
- Rules are broken

Mitigation

- Review the 'policing' and enforcement of rules
- Review the scope, nature, and effectiveness of the rules
- Review the penalties for infringement
- Consider reducing the reward level, lower rewards may reduce the incentive to cheat
- Are rewards 'winner takes all'? If so, consider tiered rewards
- Check the management behaviours exhibited. Is there tacit approval of the rule-breaking?
- Check to see if excessive management pressure is driving desperate, extreme behaviour

Contested incentive 'misses'

Symptom

- "I should have got my bonus, I was robbed!"

Mitigations

- Clear up-front explanation of the rules and rewards, including exceptions and borderline situations
- Clear, tested, and publicly available definitions and rules
- A pre-agreed neutral arbitrator can help avoid the cost and acrimony of legal action

Reward 'sticker-shock'

Symptom

- "We are paying him how much bonus?!??"

Mitigation

- Explicit warning to stakeholders at start of implementation that this may happen and is a good thing (assuming the organisational and individual benefits have been carefully aligned)
- Clear, tested, and publicly available definitions and rules
- Robust documentation of the calculations and awards to provide a clear audit trail

Rumour, innuendo and disinformation

Symptom

- "I heard those targets are to decide who to fire..."

Mitigation

- Effective launch messaging
- Honesty and trust-building
- Transparency
- Early intervention on adverse messaging

Managers abdicate responsibility, assuming incentives will manage for them

Symptom

- When issues arise, the management team immediately resort to targets and incentives to overcome the problem

Mitigation

- Incentives will only fix the issue if the target recipient has full agency (see Step 4 of ROKET-DS™). If not, extra incentives may create discontent, cheating and team tension
- For process issues, fix the process problems using a structured improvement approach before resorting to incentives

Endnotes

Endnotes

GAMED

1   Forbes, David Kiley, 'VW Executive Oliver Schmidt Sentenced To 7
    Years For Dieselgate', 6 Dec 2017.
    https://www.forbes.com/sites/davidkiley5/2017/12/06/
    vw-exec-oliver-schmidt-gets-seven-years-in-jail-for-
    dieselgate/#4e7f65545cc4

2   Mother Jones, James Grimmelmann, 'The VW Scandal Is Just the
    Beginning', 24 September 2015.
    https://www.motherjones.com/environment/2015/09/volkswagen-
    defeat-device-copyright-harry-potter/

3   The International Council on Clean Transportation, Franco,
    Vicente; Sánchez, Francisco Posada; German, John; Mock,
    Peter. 'Real-World Exhaust Emissions From Modern Diesel
    Cars' (PDF). Retrieved 26 September 2015.
    https://theicct.org/sites/default/files/publications/ICCT_PEMS-
    study_diesel-cars_20141013.pdf

4   New York Times, Bill Vlasic and Aaron M. Kessler, 'It Took E.P.A.
    Pressure to Get VW to Admit Fault', Sept 21, 2015.

5   IOPScience, Steven R H Barrett1, Raymond L Speth et al, "Impact
    of the Volkswagen emissions control defeat device on US public
    health.", Published 29 October 2015.

6   Bloomberg, Smythe, Christie, Hurtado, Patricia, 'Volkswagen
    Probed by States Over Pollution Cheating', 22 September 2015.
    https://www.bloomberg.com/news/articles/2015-09-22/
    volkswagen-probed-by-u-s-multistate-group-on-pollution-
    cheating

7   University of California - San Diego, 'Researchers find computer
    code that Volkswagen used to cheat emissions tests', 22 May 2017.
    https://phys.org/news/2017-05-code-volkswagen-emissions.html

8   NHS England, 'New ambulance service standards announced', 13
    July 2017.
    https://www.england.nhs.uk/2017/07/new-ambulance-service-
    standards-announced/

9   NHS England, 'New ambulance service standards announced', 13
     July 2017.
     https://www.england.nhs.uk/2017/07/new-ambulance-service-
     standards-announced/

10   briankellett.net, 'On how targets directly screw patient care', 5
     July 2010.
     http://www.briankellett.net/2010/07/1832/

11   CNBC, Elizabeth MacBride, 'Investment guru Charles Ellis reveals
     the ugly truth about how some funds hide poor performance that
     can derail your retirement', 19 July 2018.
     https://www.cnbc.com/2018/07/18/investment-guru-charley-ellis-
     reveals-how-funds-lie-with-statistics.html

12   S&P Dow Jones Indices, Aye M Soe, Ryan Poirier, 'SPIVA U.S.
     Scorecard', year-end 2017.
     https://www.spglobal.com/spdji/en/documents/spiva/spiva-us-
     year-end-2017.pdf

13   Source - Wikipedia, 'Grade inflation'.
     https://en.wikipedia.org/wiki/Grade_inflation

14   The Indian Express, Ritika Chopra, 6 June 2017.
     https://indianexpress.com/article/education/when-90-per-cent-
     comes-too-easy-cbse-board-exam-results-4689291/

15   The Telegraph, Graeme Paton, Sam Marsden, 21 January 2013.
     https://www.telegraph.co.uk/news/weather/9816558/Parents-hit-
     out-as-snow-shuts-more-than-5000-schools.html

16   Vanity Fair, Bethan McLean, 31 May 2017.
     https://www.vanityfair.com/news/2017/05/wells-fargo-corporate-
     culture-fraud

17   npr.org, Bill Chappell, 8 Sept 2016.
     https://www.npr.org/sections/thetwo-way/2016/09/08/493130449/
     wells-fargo-to-pay-around-190-million-over-fake-accounts-that-
     sparked-bonuses?t=1627364866727

18   Mark R. Lepper, and David Greene (1973), 'Undermining children's intrinsic interest with extrinsic reward: A test of "Overjustification" hypothesis', Journal of Personality and Social Psychology, 28(1), 129–137, Stanford University.
      https://psycnet.apa.org/record/1974-10497-001

19   Deci, E. L. (1971), The Effects of Externally Mediated Rewards on Intrinsic Motivation, April 1971Journal of Personality and Social Psychology 18(1):105-115, DOI: 10.1037/h0x0644

20   celebritynetworth.com
      https://www.celebritynetworth.com/richest-athletes/olympians/usain-bolt-net-worth/

21   thenewsmarket.com, 9 Feb 2018.
      https://www.thenewsmarket.com/news/5-things-you-need-to-know-about-olympic-timekeeping/s/a03ee86b-3c36-427a-8873-591db1255e26

22   'World Anti-Doping Agency 2018 annual report'.
      https://www.wada-ama.org/sites/default/files/resources/files/ar2018_digital_mq.pdf

23   Harvard Business Review, Motivating Salespeople: What Really Works, by Thomas Steenburgh and Michael Ahearne
      https://hbr.org/2012/07/motivating-salespeople-what-really-works

24   Wikipedia.
      https://en.wikipedia.org/wiki/Loss_aversion

25   Wikipedia.
      https://en.wikipedia.org/wiki/Pygmalion_effect

26   Lancashire Telegraph, John Anson, 15 April 2020.
      https://www.lancashiretelegraph.co.uk/news/18377624.crusher-stuff-prove-point-burnley-town-centre/

27 Harvard Business Review, Tomas Chamorro-Premuzic, 'Does money really affect motivation? A review of the research', 10 April 2013.
https://hbr.org/2013/04/does-money-really-affect-motiv

28 World Health Organization, 8 May 2020.
https://www.who.int/news-room/events/detail/2020/05/08/
default-calendar/commemorating-the-40th-anniversary-of-
smallpox-eradication

29 Fenner, Frank, Henderson, Donald A, Arita, Isao, Jezek, Zdenek, Ladnyi, Ivan Danilovich. et al. (1988). Smallpox and its eradication / F. Fenner ... [et al.]. World Health Organization.
https://apps.who.int/iris/handle/10665/39485

30 Donald R Hopkins, 'The Greatest Killer: Smallpox in History', 2002

31 Hopkins JW. The eradication of smallpox: organizational learning and innovation in international health administration. J Dev Areas. 1988 Apr;22(3):321-32. PMID: 12342353.

32 BBC News, David Shukman, 19 November 2019.
https://www.bbc.co.uk/news/science-environment-50419922

33 UK Government, 'Policy paper. Carrier bags: why there's a charge'
https://www.gov.uk/government/publications/single-use-plastic-
carrier-bags-why-were-introducing-the-charge/carrier-bags-
why-theres-a-5p-charge

34 The Guardian newspaper, Sarah Butler, 5th October 2017.
https://www.theguardian.com/uk-news/2017/oct/04/tesco-staff-
under-pressure-to-hit-financial-targets-fraud-trial-hears

35 Vanity Fair, Beth McLean, 31 May 2017.
https://www.vanityfair.com/news/2017/05/wells-fargo-corporate-
culture-fraud

36 CNN website, Greg Botelho, 27th March 2014.
https://edition.cnn.com/2014/03/27/us/air-force-cheating-
investigation/index.html

37 Vanity Fair, Bess Levin, 10 April 2017.
https://www.vanityfair.com/news/2017/04/wells-fargo-john-
stumpf-carrie-tolstedt

Endnotes

Index

Index

GAMED